MY BOY AND
AUTISM

A FATHER'S JOURNEY

KYLE WILKIN

outskirtspress
DENVER, COLORADO

Cover Photo © 2013 JupiterImages Corporation. Interior Illustrations by Katherine Collins. All rights reserved - used with permission.

Outskirts Press, Inc.
http://www.outskirtspress.com

ISBN: 978-1-4787-0468-3

Outskirts Press and the "OP" logo are trademarks belonging to Outskirts Press, Inc.

PRINTED IN THE UNITED STATES OF AMERICA

*To all the dads who had to
change their expectations abruptly*

*To our parents—Grandpa Big Deal, Grandma Kathleen,
Grandpa Ron, Grandma D, and Grandma Hough—for
doing a not-so-simple thing: listening*

*To my sister-in-law, Laura—your intelligence and genuine
interest in my project are highly treasured.
You are a gift to the Wilkin clan.*

*And, most important, to my wife, Lori—for without you,
that long walk off that short pier seems like a viable option*

HERE WE GO . . .

Preface

THANK YOU FOR joining me on my quest toward en-
lightenment on the topic of autism. Whether you are a
parent who is currently raising a child with autism or
are connected to someone who is facing these challenges, I believe my short but engaging stories will provide
a unique perspective as you delve deeper into this ex-
traordinary disorder. As you turn the pages, you'll find a
sometimes less than serious but always candid view of my
family's trials and errors in taking on autism.

I want to be clear that the opinions expressed in this
book are just that: *opinions*. They come from a regular
guy who has direct experience with this puzzling and
intriguing planet called Autism. This complex disorder
varies widely from one person to another, yet it has a
powerful and lasting effect on anyone it touches. If you
can gain any insight from this book and have a good laugh
(and maybe a moan or two), I will chalk it up as a success.
It has been a therapeutic experience to share a piece of my
topsy-turvy life with you.

Some of the names, dates, and places I mention have been
changed to protect privacy; however, the accounts in this
book are all true.

Background: A Simple Guy with a Simple Dream

I HAIL FROM the suburbs just south of San Francisco, an area known as the Peninsula. Born into a middle-income family, I was provided with three brothers, broad cultural experiences from my mother, strong character values from my father, and plenty of caring. All of this made things pretty easy for us kids. Of course, you don't always realize these insights until you have kids of your own.

For the most part, I feel like I did things right. I played recreational soccer and Little League baseball, made some close friends, stayed relatively out of trouble, graduated high school with a 3.0 GPA, and attended Chico State University for five fun-filled years. Then, after two years of "finding myself," I got a real job, married my girlfriend Lori, and became an apartment dweller in the Bay Area, not too far from the house I grew up in. After several years of scrounging and saving, Lori and I used our tiny nest egg to buy a modest home in Folsom, California. I was dialed in—job, wife, house—and ready to start a family.

I was thirty-three years old (and Lori was twenty-nine) when our first child, our daughter Riley, was born.

Having kids happened a little later in my life than I had originally intended, but everything was basically according to plan. And since we were pretty good at raising our two attention-hungry Labrador retrievers, we felt confident we'd be okay as parents.

Two years later, every father's not-so-secret dream came true for me: we had a son. *My* son.

1: It's a Boy!

A *BOY*?! COULD it be? Oh, man, was I glad I played it old-school and waited eight months, twenty-four days, six hours, and thirty-two minutes to find out the sex of our baby. "This is awesome!" I said to myself as the doctor guided—or, rather, pulled—my kid's head out. I wanted to hear the nurse say, "You have a son!" as she used that little bulb to suck out the amniotic juices from my boy's throat, but there was no missing that acorn between his legs as he arrived into the world.

Five hours later, while the rooster still slept, I was jolted awake from my uncomfortable hospital chair. "Are you ready for your son's circumcision?" asked an eager nurse.

"Uh, yeah. Sure," I said groggily as I wondered if this was all a dream. "I just need to throw some water on my face, and I'll be good to go."

Soon I was whisked away down the sterile corridors of the maternity wing. I couldn't help but think of all the choice terms I'd learned for circumcision: *take off the turtleneck sweater, give him a kosher pickle, roundhead,* and my favorite, *sharpen the pencil.* I just figured this was the thing to do. My dad did it. His dad did it. My twin brother and I had it done. It would make my son look even more like his daddy. "Okay then," I said to myself. "Let's do this common, no-big-deal, ordinary-occurrence type of thing!"

I soon found myself in the role of courageous father, peering over in what appeared to be a confused baby boy. As the doctor ceremoniously attached a peculiar metal object to my son, a bizarre sensation crept upon me as if my eyes started sweating. I instinctively began to tenderly stroke my son's arm as his tears and whines filled the room. Then, without warning, I felt like all the blood in my head had taken an unannounced and very deliberate vacation. Through a thick fog, I heard the doctor say that the procedure was over and that it looked like I could use a seat. Every one of my pores opened up. I had this odd vision that I had just performed an as-close-as-you-can-get-to-fainting-without-actually-fainting production, starring myself.

I collapsed into the nearest chair and dropped my lead-weight head between my knees. The nurses compassionately offered me cold towels for my perspiring brow, neck, and body as I did my best to put my pride back together.

Jeez-o-pete! I thought. *If I can make it through this, I can take on anything!*

Why did I ever go on and think that?! Boy, was I tempting fate. The challenges I would eventually face would pale in comparison to the event I experienced that day. Because three years and two days later, it was confirmed: my son, Aidan, had autism.

2: Hello?! Earth to Aidan!

"AIDAN." (PAUSE)

"Aidan!" (Pause)

"AIDAN!" (Pause)

What the heck? I thought.

"AIDAN!!!"

Lori came running out of the house to the backyard, where Aidan and I were in the midst of a one-way dialogue. "What's the matter?" she asked. "Why are you yelling at Aidan?"

"The boy needs his hearing checked or something," I said. "I'm just five feet behind him, and he won't even turn to look at me when I call his name."

Lori looked at me skeptically. "He had his eighteen-month appointment last week, and his ears checked out just fine."

"Well, have 'em checked again," I said.

I must admit, prior to that incident and due to my ignorance, I actually joked about Aidan's unresponsive behavior. Riley, Aidan's older sister by two years, would have a laugh about it with me too. At that time there was a children's program called *Jay Jay the Jet Plane* that had a song, "What's the Matter with Big Jake?" When Aidan would inevitably perform his apparent too-aloof-to-care act in response to our attempts to get his attention, Riley and I would sing, "What's the matter with Aidan? What's the matter with Aidan?" Of course, we didn't have a clue that he wasn't developing like a neurotypical toddler.

But then it happened—something that would set the wheels in motion for a long and challenging journey: we had our first parent-teacher conference. It would be the first of many.

Aidan's preschool teacher was very pleasant, and the meeting started out cordially. We talked about Aidan's eagerness to line up with the other children when it was playtime outside, as well as his enjoyment of finger painting. Then the language issue made its introduction. Aidan was almost two years old and was saying only three intelligible words, which we really didn't consider atypical at the time. His teacher relayed how Aidan was fairly good at answering basic questions with a "Yes," "No," or "More" response. Yet there was a definitive pause before he responded to the questions he did answer and a blank stare for the ones he did not. She also explained that Aidan did little, if anything, to communicate any needs or desires he had. He merely went with the flow of whatever was presented to him. At this point the teacher's aide, who was wiping down tables at the time, chimed in and said, "Ya know, my cousin's daughter does the same thing as Aidan, and she has autism."

The teacher looked horrified, but she managed to smooth over the aide's comment by uttering reassurances and saying she was sure everything would be fine. When the meeting concluded, we expressed our appreciation. I made my way amiably out the door, but Lori was pissed.

As soon as we reached the car, she exploded. "How dare she?! She doesn't *know* Aidan. She sees him a couple hours a day with over twenty kids in the room!"

I wasn't quite as agitated. I said, "The teacher did mention how Aidan doesn't follow along with the verbal cues at story time and doesn't show much understanding when basic instructions are given. . . ."

"I'm not talking about his teacher," she said. "I'm talking about his *aide* and the autism comment she made!"

I offered my feeble response: "Oh."

And so began the first night of our journey.

3: Night of Desperation

WELL, THAT EVENING was emotionally brutal. We spent the early part of the evening frantically surfing the Internet, typing in phrases that described Aidan's habits and behaviors. The search results kept leading us back to that dreaded word: *autism.*

In typical denial mode, we attempted to convince each other that he didn't have autism. He merely had something we came upon called mixed expressive receptive disorder. Maybe with enough speech classes, he'd be just fine. Maybe with a few summer school sessions, he'd be up there cruising with the entire class. Maybe he was just a bit behind. After all, Lori and I hadn't been fast readers or language arts geniuses, and we'd eventually caught up. Right? *Right?*

We were delusional, and we didn't know where to turn or what the heck to do. This word, *autism,* wasn't really in our vocabulary. We thought it was only used to describe people who were savants—people like the character Dustin Hoffman plays in *Rain Man.* What was our son, with no family history of these issues, doing with autism?

Lori spent the latter part of the evening on the phone with her mother, sisters-in-law, and close friends. I sat in a chair and tried to watch a baseball game on TV and tune out the frantic tones emanating from my wife in the other room. The more she talked, the more helpless I felt.

We didn't sleep much that night. This was something we should have started getting used to.

4: A Neurologist? Isn't That Brain Stuff?

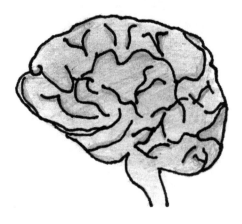

NOT KNOWING WHERE else to start, we met with Aidan's pediatrician, who basically said, "Yes, there is something going on here." He wrote out a simple referral to a neurologist, and off we went. I had only a vague idea of what a neurologist was (something to do with brains?), but I knew we'd find out soon enough, since we wasted no time in setting up an appointment.

The neurologist took about five minutes to observe Aidan while we filled him in with our take on what had been going on with our son. Then he "thoroughly" psychoanalyzed my boy by asking him a question or two and then followed up with a fifteen-minute question-and-answer period directed at us. Lori fielded all the questions because I was too preoccupied with my own thoughts to be able to contribute in any meaningful way. *What will become of Aidan's life?* I thought. *And what will become of our lives as a family?*

Dr. Humdrum seemed very unimpressed by our situation. This was a monumental, potentially life-changing situation for us, yet his demeanor was remarkably apathetic. It was as if we were seeing him for a bad case of the sniffles. I didn't expect him to be Dr. Oz, but I thought he'd have a little compassion.

Meanwhile, Aidan found a sensory-type game in the corner of the room. Contentedly busy, he pushed, pulled, and slid wooden knobs around a slotted board.

Regardless of how we felt about Dr. Nonchalant, his perfunctory examination of Aidan, and his frosty bedside manner, our future was in his hands, and he confirmed our gravest fear: Aidan had an official diagnosis of autism.

Soon Lori and I were left to process the neurologist's explanation of autism and what it meant for Aidan's future, as well as ours. In a nutshell, he told us that autism is a pervasive developmental disorder that affects the brain's social and communication skills. Because autism is a spectrum disorder, some children are more affected than others. The neurologist said we'd find out more about how the disorder would affect Aidan in the years to come, and we should watch for the following symptoms: avoiding eye contact, preferring to be by himself, no fear of danger, difficulty expressing what he wants or needs, excessive rigidity, and heightened responses to all five senses.

Lori and I were torn. On one hand, we knew the official diagnosis would allow Aidan to receive special services for therapy. On the other hand, the defeating news of so many potential deficits forced my samurai sword deeper into my gut. We had run out of excuses and denials. Now we had to face the truth.

I must point out that our pediatrician had offered us some sound advice prior to our appointment with the neurologist: "No matter the diagnosis, whatever the label given, you should try and get as many services as possible to benefit Aidan."

Our next step was to contact Alta California Regional Center. "What is that?" you might ask.

As defined by Alta:

> Alta California Regional Center is an agency that assists with coordinating the services and supports that are necessary for persons with developmental disabilities to maximize and increase their opportunities and choices.
>
> Alta California Regional Center comes along side other community agencies to assist in filling in any gaps that exist in a consumer's total constellation of life goals and assessed needs.
>
> Alta California Regional Center is a place where families and consumers can bring their ideas, needs, plans and wishes to a team of professionals who partner with the family and consumer to set achievable goals and to assess and determine the best way to meet those goals.

Alta California Regional Center is an agency that believes in pursuing the least restrictive settings and services for consumers, and believes in long-range planning to achieve the least restrictive, most inclusive lifestyle possible for each individual consumer, based on each consumer's individual strengths and challenges.[1]

As translated by me in regards to Aidan:

Alta has been a key player in improving life opportunities for Aidan through a plethora of therapies.

Unfortunately, however, Alta didn't honor our neurologist's diagnosis of autism. In fact, our Alta representative rolled her eyes when we told her which neurologist we had gone to. (Jeez! Where else were we supposed to go? He was the only neurologist who diagnosed autism within a thirty-mile radius!)

Another downer was that Alta had to do their own battery of tests on Aidan to establish their own diagnosis. There was a three-month waiting list for such an appointment, and then we had to wait another three months to wait for the results. Only after that could we launch a therapy game plan for Aidan.

In all, it took about a year to receive any substantial services leading us down Aidan's "road to recovery," for the lack of a better term. Alta is not a great place for the impatient, but it is a fantastic government program for which we are forever grateful. In the end, documentation

---

1 http://www.altaregional.org/about/whatIsAlta/

from our initial appointments with Aidan's pediatrician and neurologist permitted him to receive occupational therapy (OT) and speech and language services in a timelier manner.

Now the frustration would begin for all of us.

5: I ♥ Someone with AUTISM

BEFORE I GET into the details of our whirlwind therapy
tour with Aidan, let me tell you a little about some of our
newfound coping mechanisms.

Within a week of the diagnosis, Lori embraced the
news with vigor. Her vehicle for information, and her
newest and bestest buddy, was the computer. She joined
two online forums on autism, bookmarked seven autism
websites, and purchased an I ♥ SOMEONE WITH AUTISM tote
bag, as well as a license plate frame bearing the same
rainbow-colored motto.

I, on the other hand, didn't join in the kumbaya love-
fest so quickly. I was still reeling from the notion that my
boy might never go to college, never get married, and possibly never enjoy a good game of catch with his old man.

I must admit, I was impressed with the way Lori handled the situation. It wasn't as if I buried my head in the sand and just waited for the world to go away, but she was able to skip to the next chapter of our lives more gracefully than I could ever imagine. She was very open about autism with our family and friends; she'd discuss the topic candidly and share all the gritty details. By contrast, I sent a sincere yet nonspecific email to a couple of my closest pals to inform them of our situation.

Lori's eagerness to ride the autism bandwagon eventually rubbed off on me, and I opened up about our situation with a few of my coworkers. I've never been one to unload my emotional burdens on people outside my family, but it did feel good to share a thought or two about what was going on in my life instead of looking at it as a dark family secret.

Learning to talk about it helped, but I also subconsciously made a mental shift, thrusting myself further into the role of Family Man. While Lori bought more I ♥ SOMEONE WITH AUTISM paraphernalia online, Family Man purchased custom-made attire to demonstrate his dedication. I proudly sported a shirt emblazoned with stick figures of my wife, kids, and dogs for the entire nation to see. Sure, my friendly colleagues gave me a hard time about my newly revealed self-absorption, but I didn't care. I was *in it to kin it!* (Trademark!) And I was forcing myself to come out of the closet with respect to autism.

6: A Third Child: Are You Kidding Me?!

WHEN I CAME home from work I had a strange feeling, as if the stars were either all aligned or totally out of whack. Something was oddly tense as I peered into the open door of the guest bathroom. Here I observed the consoling posture of Lori's mom as she attempted to dry the overflowing tears of her daughter, my wife.

They turned simultaneously in my direction and met my perplexed stare. And then I caught sight of the stick Lori held in her quivering fingers: the unplanned conception of our third child had occurred.

Now, I'm no champion of controversial subjects, but I will admit that the word *abortion* raced through my mind. I've always been a silent proponent of a couple's right to choose, but it was mostly at a hypothetical, philosophical level. I never thought I'd actually be faced with this type of quandary. Heck, I was married—unplanned pregnancies were the problems of teenagers and single folks, right?

Yet, at that moment, a strange feeling erupted within my soul. Maybe it was the calamitous look in Lori's eyes. But I calmly said, without reservation, "We'll be okay. We'll have this baby. This is a good thing. A blessed thing. We'll be okay."

I must have said "We'll be okay" a dozen times in my quest to dry Lori's tears. At the same time, I was also trying to convince myself that we were going to survive this huge serving of bombshell pie. The cruel facts were these: I was a teacher with a modest income, the monthly bills were already hard to manage, and our children, at ages four (Riley) and two (Aidan), had unique sets of issues that needed tending to. From that moment on, though, I never looked back, nor did I have any regrets about having a third child.

One element that I hadn't counted on in our childbearing years was the severe hit they had on my wife's body image. I certainly didn't mind Lori's metamorphic physical frame; I love her for *her*, and I would tell her it's just more of her that I get to love, even if she's not always fond of my teasing. But based on her experience birthing our two other kids, it was evident that she was the "bloating" type. By the thirty-second week of both her prior pregnancies, Lori ballooned up like the girl in the *Willy Wonka* movie who inflates into a huge blueberry, causing the Oompa Loompas to roll her out the door to the juicing room. (Sorry, sweetheart, but it's true.)

The tragic, and somewhat ironic, part of the story is that a year after Aidan was born, Lori decided she was ready to lose some weight and joined Weight Watchers. She dedicated many loyal months to the program, and just when she told me that she was beginning to feel healthy and better about herself with the weight loss, the news of our third child's impending arrival came along—and there went any hope of Lori deservedly putting herself first for anything for a while.

Body image issues aside, it was a really a tough time for us. The jokes of Lori being Fertile Myrtle were harmless, of course. But with the question marks about Aidan's development looming, our supportive sets of parents living hours away, and dreams of monthly college fund contributions rapidly evaporating, we were a bit dismayed at what we had created for ourselves.

But Lori and I are positive people, and we have faith that things always work out for the best. We continue to tell ourselves that things happen for a reason (even though I'm still coming to terms with my son's situation). And many years from now, like when I'm enjoying a round of golf at age seventy, I'll never have to contemplate any what-ifs in regards to my youngest daughter.

Even now, nine years into parenthood, we know we haven't got it all figured out just yet. What we do know is that the birth of our third and *last* child was definitely a gift and a blessing. Kira is now a bright, neurotypical, and boisterous five-year old little girl. While she's certainly a pistol, we couldn't imagine not having this little person in charge (so she thinks). Besides being Aidan's sister, she is his best friend. She is starting to guide him with appropriate engagement techniques, while also offering him all the bossiness a little sister can dish out.

When I see them love each other (and argue, as siblings do), I tell Lori, "You know, people pay big money to have their special-needs child experience this kind of social play." She's probably heard me say that a hundred times now, but I don't think it bothers her at all.

7: The Land of Occupational Therapy: A Lighthearted Review

IF YOU'VE NEVER been to an OT clinic, you really should buy a ticket.

On our first visit, after Aidan (two and a half years old at the time) made thirtysomething handprints on the lobby fish tank, a spirited young woman magically appeared in the doorway leading to the inner office. Mia introduced herself and led us to a wondrous land: the Land of OT.

Remember that scene from *Willy Wonka & the Chocolate Factory* (This was a popular movie in our house at this time), when the group is walking down the hallway that gets smaller and smaller and finally a tiny door opens up into that gigantic room where everything is a colorful and tasty surprise to the senses? Entering the Land of OT felt a little like that.

Upon entering, I observed a young boy, about six years old, lying facedown with his stomach on a scooter-type board with a long rope attached to it. The other end of the rope was in the hands of a robust, animated gal who was towing him around the room. This therapist seemed to have the strength of a bodybuilder and the enthusiastic facial expressions of a sidewalk mime. The more she bobbed her head with wide-grinned approval, the more the boy kicked his feet and "swam" his arms over the floor to help propel himself.

I felt my own (self-diagnosed) ADD kicking in as my attention was drawn to a little girl of about four years old, who was happily swinging in a chair-like hammock suspended from the ceiling. Actually, it was more like she was frantically spinning. Her OT would energetically clap her hands with every rotation and subsequent moment of eye contact. The girl's tornado activity was even more interesting because of the large headphones she wore. I glanced at Aidan's OT and sheepishly motioned to the smiling girl's puffy earmuffs as if to say, "Will my kid be rockin' out to my favorite 80s bands during his session too?"

She nonchalantly replied, "Oh, that's called listening therapy. I can discuss that with you after Aidan's session." (I'll share my thoughts on listening therapy in another chapter.)

Mia guided us to a back room and briefly explained that I was welcome to sit in on this first thirty-minute session, but future meetings would be more productive if I waited in the lobby. Then she had Aidan sit in a pint-size chair at a miniature table and asked him if he'd like to play with a special type of play-dough called Theraputty.

Mia explained that she was evaluating Aidan's sensory needs and that this type of activity could help him regulate himself at home if he was craving some sensory input.

I should mention here that, by this point in time, I was regularly learning new terms: *sensory input, sensory integration, neurotypical, listening therapy, ADD, ADHD, Asperger's,* and more. I felt I had come so far in my education that I could just about keep up with any conversation having to do with special-needs issues, and I had a pretty realistic understanding of autism. But that was naive.

When I heard Mia mention that Aidan could learn to "regulate himself" at home, a big, glaring lightbulb went on in my head. Based on what I'd learned in those first five minutes in OT (and on my own simplistic and desperate thought process about autism), I thought, *That's it! I can get Aidan a heavy punching bag. I'll hang it in the garage and have him pound that thing every day, whereby he'll self-regulate. Aidan will punch out his autism! Cured!*

See what I mean? Still gullible, simplistic, desperate. It took me a few weeks before I came back to my senses and realized how foolish I was. Unfortunately, autism is a little more perplexing than the need to hit a punching bag.

Well, back to the Theraputty . . .

Aidan quickly probed, prodded, and squeezed the *Thera* out of that *putty.* According to Mia, Aidan was currently seeking tactile stimulation. Apparently some kids crave it, while others may be defensive to it. In this case, Aidan was obviously a craver.

A few minutes into this activity, Mia added pennies into the mix. She pushed them into the putty and instructed Aidan to get them out. Afterward he was to push the pennies back in himself. Aidan seemed to really enjoy this. *Cool!* I thought. *Therapy is going to be a breeze.*

Wrong again.

Mia put the putty away and started the next activity: hand-over-hand line drawing. It began with Aidan's feeble attempt to draw a line with a pencil, from one dot on the page to another. Mia demonstrated by putting her hand over Aidan's and guiding the pencil in the direction of the second dot, but apparently Aidan didn't grasp the concept. He grabbed the pencil like an angry monkey squeezing a banana out of its peel and proceeded to scrawl a wavy line that didn't quite reach its intended destination. Mia started again, patiently guiding the pencil with her hand over Aidan's, but I could already see where this was going. The waves of Aidan's sea suddenly turned violent as Mia continued her test of the hand-over-hand technique that, frankly, infuriated Aidan.

Then, from out of nowhere, a high-pitched screeching sound emitted from deep within Aidan: "Noooo!!!" With a jerking pull, he yanked the pencil away from Mia's grasp.

> *The parents of Aidan Wilkin cordially invite you
> to the debut performance of Aidan's stubborn disposi-
> tion when receiving vital educational life skills.*

Whoa, tiger! I thought. *What the heck happened here?*
Aidan was content as a squirrel with a walnut when playing
with the putty stuff, but the next thing you know he's flipping
out when offered physical assistance with a writing utensil.

Mia calmly pointed out that Aidan had a "minor"
stubborn quality but that it wasn't "that bad."

"We'll just have to work through it," she said.

Minor? In my view he was out of control, and I didn't
like it. How this lady could be so patient in response to
his outburst was beyond me. Later, however, I came to
respect the composure of these professionals during these
moments of emotional expressiveness, to put it mildly.

Part of me wanted to force my kid into submission,
while the other wanted to drag my child out the door due
to my own frustration.

After a few more attempts of the Mia's-hand-of-
persistence-over-Aidan's-death-grip lesson, Mia asked
Aidan, "Would you like to play with the beans?"

Aidan responded with the same look as Daddy's
(blank), but he didn't say no. So Mia reached behind her,
took a shoebox-size tub of dried pinto beans off the shelf,
and placed it before Aidan. She demonstrated by putting
her hands into the wondrous tub of tactile freedom, and
then she eased Aidan's hands into the box.

Aidan's eyes lit up, and his grumpy, sulky demeanor morphed into a blissful display of delight. His smile grew by the second, and it was clear that he loved this tactile experience. Mia smiled and ended our session a few minutes later. Next time, she said, we'd see how Aidan liked sitting in a large tub of beans.

Holy cow! I thought. *The boy will be in sensory heaven!*

Later that day I was at the market buying twenty bags of pinto beans and a large plastic tub to initiate the transformation of our living room into our sensory room. Yes, it was a mess. And yes, I occasionally pulled beans out of Aidan's nose. But both he and his older sister loved the sensory room nonetheless.

A few days later, we showed up for our second OT appointment. It began with twisting and turning in the chair hammock, similar to what I had seen the little girl experience a few days earlier. Aidan was hesitant at first, but soon he was in his element. His sensory cravings were joyfully being saturated with every rock and turn.

And so it went. From session to session his therapists molded his will to try new things. Once Aidan entered kindergarten, his school took over his OT program, and Aidan began to receive therapy there just once a week. This was okay with us, for he had plenty of other therapies to fill his day.

8: Speech and Language Training: We Were Not Alone

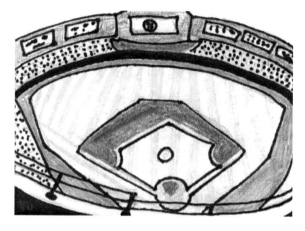

AS I MENTIONED earlier, Aidan qualified right away for speech and language services in addition to OT. But before he could receive speech therapy from Sheila, a highly recommended speech and language provider, Lori and I had to attend a two-month training course, meeting one night a week for three hours.

So we found a sitter for the first session, and off we went. Running about ten minutes late (the usual Wilkin time), we entered the large home of Sheila's mother, where we sat in a jumbled assortment of secondhand chairs arranged in a circle in the living room. I immediately claimed the cushiony one—chivalry was not a priority for this three-hour affair. Sitting in the other relics were the most puzzled, deer-in-headlights looks ever seen on parents' faces. They looked how we felt: helpless and clueless.

Sheila promptly got us engaged by having us introduce ourselves and create an artsy project pertaining to our children. Basically, we wrote and decorated Aidan's name with colored markers on a poster board. Then we came up with descriptive adjectives for each letter in his name. Soon all the parents eagerly presented highlights on their tots as Sheila made the transition to the next stage of her language program.

During Sheila's class, not once did she use any labels about our children. This helped her avoid striking fear in this emotionally fragile crowd of parents. Instead she used politically correct terms like *language delayed* and *linguistically challenged* to describe our "future NASA scientists," as she liked to imply. She provided several suggestions on how to engage our children in talking more. For example, she said, "Get your children to *ask* for what they want, rather than simply assuming and getting it for them. Put that sippy cup or box of trains on a high shelf so you can get them saying *cup* and *train*, thus communicating and working for what they want with language." Sheila told us not to be too concerned with perfect pronunciation in the beginning. She said we should expect some frustration but assured us that the engagement strategies would eventually work. Getting our kids to use their voices was the first hurdle.

I was really impressed with this commonsense approach to drawing out speech in Aidan. He usually

waddled on over to the refrigerator and stood there await-
ing our butler-esque services. I'd typically rattle off the
available provisions until he nodded. Then he'd get what
he wanted and stroll off without a word. Now he'd have
to *earn* the things he wanted—with language.

We applied this new technique almost immediately
at home, and we quickly saw some results. It worked for
just about anything. Aidan was now asking for his truck
("truh") and his train ("tray").

At subsequent meetings, Sheila helped us refine our
techniques and added new ways for us to bring about
more speech and better pronunciation of words from our
little sponges by using just the right balance of push-and-
pull tactics.

As the weeks progressed, we parents got a little more
comfortable with each other. Our walls of judgment about
each other and our children were collapsing, and we began
to share intimate stories of our successes and struggles at
fostering our children's development. For example, Lori
shared how Aidan was in occupational therapy and explained how it was helping him request objects with fewer
outbursts. Another parent described how her son Andrew
recently had begun a tumbling class to support his desire
to bump into things. She further explained that the chance
to roll and bounce around for forty-five minutes seemed
to aid Andrew in talking afterward. But all this constructive dialogue changed on our last week of training, when
our conversations took on a little less sugar and a lot more
spice.

Sheila gave us plenty of time to discuss some learning strategies, and before long, the dreaded labels started to flow from the parents: autism, Asperger's, ADD, ADHD, Down's, communicatively handicapped, pervasive development disorder, and so on. You could feel the hyperawareness of each parent kick in.

It was interesting to see the internal conflicts that surfaced. Some parents began to take a guarded approach to the information about each condition, while others were completely open and shared details I'd normally reserve for only our closest relatives. One couple seemed to be in denial about the obvious deficits of their child. I recall them going into a figurative fetal position and vehemently denying that their child had anything beyond a speech delay. And yet, this parent also shared that his kid was in OT for some sensory defensiveness and lack of eye contact—both of which are common symptoms of autism.

Others were pouring out details as if they were releasing their welled-up concerns.

"My child eats bark, and my sister says Jeremy may have pica," said one mother.

"Suzy talks a mile a minute reciting *Blue's Clues,* and my father says its something called echolalia," said another.

"Tanner won't eat anything but crackers and water."

"Why does Ricky intentionally crash into doors and walls?"

"Does this sound like Asperger's?"

"Is ADD on the autistic spectrum?"

Unanswered questions kept flying.

Geez, are we as neurotic as these parents? I thought.

Almost all parents would close their comments with something positive about their kids:

"Ahmed is starting to pronounce his Ts."

"Alexa is so loving toward her baby sister."

"Logan has improved so much since two weeks ago."

And so it continued until Sheila regrouped us.

The fact of the matter is that we all cared deeply about our cherubs, but we were all equally frustrated at the lack of any exact answers on how to fix our little ones' deficits.

Sheila seemed to sense these feelings, and she offered encouraging words to soothe our troubled hearts and minds. I remember speaking to her one-on-one later that evening, and while she was careful not to brand any child with a label, she left me with a very positive thought: "He'll probably be an engineer someday." While I didn't think anyone on my side of the family had the critical thinking skills to be a mechanical, chemical, or industrial engineer, I meekly nodded in the hope that maybe my kid had a chance. A chance is what all the parents of special-needs kids—or any kids, for that matter—desire.

As we approached our car, I was about to share what Sheila had said with Lori when one of the other mothers approached us. She gushed optimistically.

"I am so relieved," she said. "I was so concerned about my lil' Jorge, and Sheila said not to worry and that he'll probably be an architect someday. Do you really think he can?"

I felt like throwing my hands up in the air and saying, "Yeah, and I heard from the same lady that my kid would someday be designing rockets. . . . Who knows?!" Instead I squared my body toward her and declared in my most sincere and reassuring voice, "Yes, he'll probably build ballparks."

She let out a nervous but happy giggle, then anxiously searched her purse for her keys as we drove off into the night.

I didn't have the heart to tell Lori about the engineer comment until later.

9: Listening Therapy: "Ouch, My Ears! Something Is Horribly Out of Tune!"

WHENEVER THERE WAS a loud noise, such as a high volume on the television or a fire engine siren blaring by, Aidan would desperately clap his hands over his ears like an old man being forced to listen to the latest hit rap song. We brought up this issue with Aidan's occupational therapist, Mia, and she said, "Listening therapy—not to be confused with music therapy—is sometimes introduced to alleviate a child's sensitivity to certain sounds." (She always had a way of relaying information in a manner that did not make us adults feel clueless.)

As soon as Lori and I got home, we googled "listening therapy," just as we'd done for all other topics having to do with autism. We found an excess of random information regarding the use of listening therapy.

For example, one website recommended that a child listen to the same CD for thirty minutes twice a day for a designated period of time—say, two weeks—and then follow up with another CD from the set for another two weeks, and then another, and so on. This technique was said to promote the following characteristics:

- focus and concentration
- spatial awareness and body movement
- language skills
- social skills (such as turn taking)
- self-regulation
- academic ability
- calmness
- sensory modulation (i.e., anything to do with the five senses)

"Wow!" I said facetiously. "Aidan will be *rehabilitated* in a matter of weeks!"

We'd agreed to stop fantasizing about any magical cures and had given up that notion within a year of Aidan's diagnosis. We have *never* dismissed an opportunity to try something that might help our son, however.

So, with cautious interest, we asked the school's occupational therapist to order some CD's for us. And then we headphoned Aidan as prescribed.

I have always believed that if you are going to try any nontraditional therapy on your child, you should first use yourself as a guinea pig in your well-intended experiment. And that's just what I did.

"Ahhh . . ." I said as I placed the expensive CD in my daughter's music player and read from the cover on the case. "Mozart's finest music. And *modulated,* too, whatever that means."

I administered the new, sixty-dollar, Internet-ordered headphones (because the ten-dollar drugstore set apparently couldn't support the enhanced frequencies of our modulated CD) to my classic rock–fed ears and turned the volume up to a generous level.

It seemed harmless enough. The sounds of many string instruments I couldn't even name filled my head with a rhythmic yet soothing melody. Very pleasant. I could practically feel the synapses in my brain clicking together in new and enlightening ways. So far, so good! Then, about ten seconds into the song . . .

"YEEEOOOWWW! What the bleepin' bleep was that?!" A shrill, piercing pulse of noise punched through my eardrums for a split second, like a crystal vase being smashed with a sledgehammer. A couple of mellow harpsichord and cello vibrations later, it happened again. And again. And again! It was now evident to me what the term modulation meant. The music had distinct changes in pitch and volume that made it fairly uncomfortable to tolerate when hearing it for the first time.

I felt like there were waves and pulsations traveling across the backs of my eyeballs. I quickly turned the volume down a few decibels and regained my composure.

After about two minutes of enduring this strange new "music," I was able to manage the disruptive and unpredictable tones quite well.

You can bet I called Lori in from the other room to have her give it a try. I greeted her with a sinister smile and handed her the goods.

"Your turn, sweetheart."

She listened, but didn't show anything close to the stunned response that I'd had. *Interesting.*

She casually said, "Oh, yeah, I hear it now. It's just like Mia said. There are higher and lower frequencies set in the music. It's supposed to help with Aidan's hypersensitivity to sound, and may calm him some." And with this hands-on parental research, we began Aidan's listening therapy program.

Aidan wore that disco-style headset everywhere: on the way to speech therapy, after occupational therapy, on the way to school, on the drive to the park, while playing with his trains, while drawing pictures, and at many other spare moments in his hectic schedule.

You may be wondering, "Well, did all those CDs work for you?"

They kind of worked. It was difficult to live up to the twice-a-day routine for the period of time that was theoretically required. I do believe that the technique lessened Aidan's sensitivity to sounds and noises in crowded areas (for example, a swarm of enthusiastic kids waiting at the top of a playground slide). As for the focus and attention benefits, I'm not totally convinced.

I compare the CD program to allergy shots. When I was twelve, I was horribly allergic to weeds, grasses, and trees. I could always tell when baseball season was approaching, because I'd feel like I had a head cold for weeks at a time. My mother would drag my brother and me to the local allergy clinic a couple times a week for allergy shots in the arm and generous prescriptions for anti-itch cream that didn't work worth a darn. We'd repeat the procedure once a week for several weeks. Each week they'd slightly increase the dosage of antigen, and we'd gradually adjust to it.

And so it was with listening therapy. Whatever frequency of sounds Aidan resisted, he got a tolerable daily dose until he adapted to it. Rocket science? Maybe not, but it's a pretty good idea in theory. And even after all the other therapies and rigamarole we've routinely put Aidan through, we still go back to listening therapy once in a while. There are random days or even weeks when Aidan will suddenly get sensitive to noises and say, "That's too louuuud" or "It hurts my earrrs," followed by the hands-over-the-ears drama. But really, it's not theatrics. We've learned that children on the autistic spectrum are simply hypersensitive to certain sounds.

We find that an occasional routine of listening therapy for thirty minutes, twice a day, for one to two weeks, usually chills Aidan out amid the external clatter that most people naturally adjust to.

10: Physical Therapy:
The Informed and the Uninformed

ABOUT THE TIME we were dealing with the news from Alta that Aidan (now almost three years old) was indeed on the autistic spectrum, I noticed some physical peculiarities about him. Specifically, when he walked, he held his right arm in a slightly flexed position. And, come to think of it, he tripped a lot too.

I told Lori about this, and she said, "I guess so. I really haven't noticed. You're the PE teacher." (It's true. I am a physical education teacher.)

And just like that, another round of doctor appointments was set in motion. (We were on a first-name basis with our pediatrician by now.) Soon, we were referred to our uncharismatic neurologist, who subsequently referred us to a clinic that did MRIs (magnetic resonance imaging), to see if Aidan had cerebral palsy.

If you've never had the distinct pleasure of holding down your special-needs child in order for a stranger to stick him with a sharp object, you've been fortunate. Lori and I had that enjoyable experience just prior to the MRI. Since we couldn't expect Aidan to lie perfectly still for the procedure, the idea was to have him sleep through it, which could be accomplished only with a little medicinal assistance. Aidan wasn't interested in getting a shot, and he emphatically refused the needle in his arm, so we had to wrestle him into submission. It wasn't fun. He muffled the words he'd been learning in speech: "No-theng-you. No-theng-you." There was a definite edge of panic in his voice.

When we finally got him still enough to proceed, the commanding yet gentle nurse calmly stated, "It will be no more than ten seconds before Aidan will drift off to a sound sleep."

She wasn't kidding! As soon as we saw the sleepy fluid enter his system through a narrow plastic tube, all of the no-theng-yous sailed off into the horizon. The pendulum-like sway of his head ceased, and he closed his heavy eyelids. Aidan was at peace and now ready for the brain scan. (And yes, I asked the nurse, like everyone else does, "Where can I get some of that stuff?")

Three days later, Dr. Insensitive, our neurologist, explained that the MRI clearly showed a small white speck on Aidan's brain, and that it had formed while he was in utero. He further clarified that the formation of this speck was similar to having a stroke, and it impacted Aidan's motor skills. We certainly speculated about whether there was a connection between autism and Aidan's newly confirmed ailment, but my research revealed no link. However, I did find that people with autism usually have some other underlying issues, such as epilepsy (a disorder associated with seizures) or gastrointestinal disorders. Thankfully, Aidan doesn't pad his stat sheet with any further conditions that we are aware of. But the MRI confirmed that Aidan had a mild form of cerebral palsy (CP).

Oh, joy. Another diagnosis, I thought. *How could this have happened?* I hadn't initially questioned the autism diagnosis much, but I did have trepidations about CP, and I kept trying to pinpoint the cause. The only thing I could think of was the fact that Lori's stepfather had died while she was pregnant with Aidan, and I knew Lori had had a really tough time dealing with that. That was just wild speculation on my part, though. Who knows how the miniature stroke could have happened?

What I did know, at this stage of the game, was that I wasn't going to get anywhere worrying about why, so I put aside my mental list of potential causes and focused on what I could do for my boy.

We were then referred to physical therapy (PT) for Aidan. At this point, Aidan was already receiving speech and OT services, and I was wondering if there was a one-stop shop for all the therapies he needed. After all, we had merely scratched the surface of the services Alta had available.

Suitably, Aidan's OT place offered PT too. And I later discovered that, at least in Aidan's case, OT took care of any sensory issues and small-motor skills (such as holding an object appropriately), while PT handled large-motor movement. So, PT seemed to be a natural step in his progression.

Aidan was actually taking all his therapies in stride. Lori and I tag-teamed it, transporting him from OT to speech and now to PT. He happily played on the McDonald's PlayPlace structure for speech days and eagerly made sand piles at the park after trips to OT. We continued to create a fun atmosphere by letting him jump himself silly in a warehouse of inflatable bounce houses on PT days.

At his first PT appointment, Aidan was set up with a young, physically able woman named Taylor. She immediately got him moving by placing him in a ball pit (a ten-by-ten-foot box filled with soft plastic balls). She then had him climb stairs in locomotor fashion (left-right, left-right), which was helpful because Aidan normally led with his left foot up every step.

Taylor was good at her craft, and she understood the challenges faced by kids with autism. I was impressed with her firm hand and tone, which Aidan needed. She was patient but still provided the essential boundaries.

After four sessions, Taylor informed me that Aidan's condition was very mild and that PT is mainly for people who really need help walking and getting around, so Aidan's PT services would be limited. I wasn't that broken up by the news, but I was bummed that he was going to miss some teacher-directed development. Aidan was clearly an active, rough-and-tumble kid who had difficulty making transitions from one activity to the next. I was okay with him losing the dynamic physical play but mildly disappointed that he would also be discontinuing the behavioral-development side of the sessions. He still needed help with obediently following instructions.

Taylor did agree to recommend four more sessions in her evaluation, but that would most likely conclude Aidan's physical therapy. I looked at it as a farewell gift, since Taylor, unfortunately for us, went on vacation.

I say "unfortunately" because Aidan was reassigned to Hilda, an older lady who appeared to be pushing seventy. She appeared uncharacteristically fragile and meek for this type of work and visibly lacked the confidence that Taylor had projected.

Hilda calmly greeted an eager Aidan in the lobby. He was ready to attack the crater of balls he had explored during the previous session and enthusiastically went through the door. By this point in his therapy, I was confined to the reception area, where, once again, just as in the numerous OT sessions, I stared glassy-eyed at that hypnotic fish tank. There's something so calming about that fish tank.

Five minutes into Aidan's session, I was abruptly shaken from my happy place. Hilda opened the lobby door and said abrasively, "Aidan is being noncompliant. He's throwing temper tantrums, and I'm finding it hard to move him."

I sat there feeling perplexed. I was thinking, *What do you mean, you can't move him? He's three years old! Force him if you need to, you old trout. You have my complete support. I grant you full authority to do what you need to do to get the job done.*

But what I said was, "Yes, ma'am. Would you like my assistance?"

Hilda desperately replied, "Yes!"

I soon realized Hilda could not move Aidan at all. She was physically slight and lacked the strength necessary to deal with a kid like him.

When I explained to her that Aidan's autism made transitions to other activities difficult, it became obvious why Hilda was experiencing so much difficulty. Her response was telling.

"What's autism?" she asked.

I guess it wasn't Hilda's fault. She wasn't educated in this area, and the person who assigned her to Aidan should have been aware of this. From Hilda's perspective, she thought Aidan was being ornery and ill-mannered. This experience taught me that not all therapists who deal with special-needs children possess a knowledge base about autism.

Accordingly, I had Aidan reassigned to a more informed and, coincidentally, less "seasoned" physical therapist. But our adventures in PT Land were scheduled to draw to a close after three more sessions anyway, so I tried not to worry about his assignment too much after that.

To this day Aidan has a bit of a crook to his arm that I probably notice more than anyone else. But he doesn't fall down quite as often as he did before, if at all. With many summers of diving into the pool, daily jumping off the couch, and wrestling matches with Daddy, he has improved his coordination and balance on his own. The everyday physical activity helps, but I do believe Aidan's love of swimming has been the greatest factor in his victories over cerebral palsy.

11: What's the Matter, Aidan?

THE DISORDER OF autism has presented itself in heart-wrenching ways, for Lori and me as well as for Aidan. When your four-year-old child cannot express himself with words to tell you how he feels, you are often at a loss for how to ease his pain. Here's a brief story illustrating that point.

"Time for bed!" I yelled down the hallway to my crazy woodchucks, who were creating movable art out of chairs and cushions (as well as creating a mess, in addition to the one Lori and I had just cleaned up the hour before).

Lori and I hustled each resisting child into the bathroom in an attempt to commence the nightly hand-washing and tooth-brushing ritual, which none of the kids can seem to get used to. Finally, we corralled them to their bedrooms. (Kira and Riley share their sisterly dormitory, and Prince Aidan has a cabana to himself.)

On a typical night, if it's not too late and I haven't passed out from exhaustion yet, I'll read a story to Aidan in his bed, or he'll read it to me. Pretty good for a kid who cannot speak well and seems not to comprehend much around him. (In truth, at this stage, Aidan's not really reading word for word. He has simply memorized sets of words on each page. But when I want to get to my own siesta in a timely manner, forget the double-page-skip trick. He's too sly for that one.)

On this particular night, I noticed Aidan seemed a bit melancholy. *He must have had a long day*, I thought. After all, he'd gone to school, followed by four hours of ABA (applied behavior analysis), and probably had received at least speech, listening, food, physical, or playgroup therapy too. Then Dad had drilled him with more questions to close out his day. *The boy is probably drained.*

I gave him a hug and kiss goodnight and said, "I love you, Aidan."

Usually I get a scripted "I love you" right back before he rolls over to burrow his head in his cushy pillow. But this time I didn't. Instead I heard a weak moan that sounded like it came from a wounded animal.

"What's the matter, Aidan?" I said with a perplexed look on my face.

Aidan glanced woefully at me and moaned again.

Now my worry set in to match his sadness, and I said compassionately, "What's going on? What's wrong, buddy?"

Aidan made an incoherent mumble as his bottom lip started to shudder.

At this point I felt helpless. Aidan could neither express his feelings nor communicate key words to let me know what was wrong. I called for Lori, who was putting down the girls, and continued my cross-examination of Aidan.

"Are you hurt?" I asked, peering into his eyes as if I could penetrate his thoughts.

"Yessssss," he said in barely a whisper.

Jeez-o! Couldn't he just tell me what was up? I was dyin' here!

Then Mommy walked in and tried the same telepathic stare that I had attempted a moment before.

"Touch your boo-boo for me, pal," I said in desperation.

Aidan glanced at Mommy and tucked his chin. Then his eyes welled up, and he pressed his top lip to his protruding bottom one. He kept his head down as he raised his puppy-dog eyes and placed his hand over his heart.

Lori said, "Ohhhh, sweetheart. I'm sorry." She immediately made her way toward him.

My split-second, dense-guy thought: *Huhhh?* Another pause, then: *Ohhhh, he wants his mommy.*

Lori gave Aidan a big hug as he buried his cheek against her bosom.

I heard a gentle sigh of relief from Lori and a deep, relaxed breath from Aidan. He was asleep in seconds.

12: *A* Is for *Apple*;
I Is for the *Importance of Speech*

IF I HAD plenty of cash, I'd provide my kid with one-on-one, private-practice speech and language tutoring five days a week. Unfortunately, like most people in this country, we aren't independently wealthy.

Lori and I knew in our hearts that Aidan's communication skills were the key to his success in and out of school. And for most children with autism, speech and language deficits rear their problematic heads early. These symptoms can include a very limited vocabulary, a high-pitched and robotic tone of voice, and difficulty understanding very basic questions.

From the beginning stages of preschool, Aidan's speech and language limitations became more and more obvious. For example, when other children in his age group began forming complete sentences, he still had a hard time with the endings of simple words. We were aware that he was delayed, but due to his autism, his learning curve was much slower than we projected. He was speaking as if he were hearing impaired. Words like *thank* and *help* faded before he reached the defining last letter or two. Aidan's speech took me back to my own high school days when my father would say, "E-NUN-CI-ATE YOUR WORDS." Now I found myself trying to help my son pronounce his words with clarity too. Reminders from my parents fixed my issue, however: Aidan's disabilities required intensive therapy beyond what we had learned from Sheila's parent-training classes—and beyond my instructions to enunciate..

One of our main concerns was that in a school setting, Aidan wouldn't be able to express his needs verbally. He wouldn't be able to say that he was without something, like a pencil. Or that he needed to go to the bathroom. Or that he had gotten hurt on the playground at recess. Our minds raced with negative thoughts about his educational future. Expressive language became our primary focus for Aidan's therapy.

A historic and infamous incident illustrating Aidan's limited verbal skills happened when he was four. We took a father-and-son trip to the grocery store. This was an all-important mission for an essential item that Daddy really needed: beer. I knew that Aidan was shy, especially in unchartered surroundings, so I usually kept our outings more structured and planned—for instance, an afternoon of specific activities at the park. So when we made our approach to the grocery store's automatic sliding entry-way doors, it was no surprise that, given Aidan's clenched fingers, I was in for a treat. His body language told me that he wasn't fired up about the idea of going inside, and his verbal feedback had remnants of his MRI days: "No thengs 'n' thengs" ("No thanks").

I pretended that I hadn't heard him as I managed to pull him through the doorway. And despite his dramatic moaning and groaning, I did my best to coax him to take a ride in the shopping cart. I could feel the number of glances increase as onlookers witnessed this father hoisting a reluctant little boy into his mobile metal cage. After I got his transporter moving, however, Aidan seemed to enjoy the ride.

We cruised past the colorful produce section, which lit up Aidan's eyes, and made our way closer to Daddy's destination. But before we could turn the final corner, Aidan made a play at some cheap hanging toys on the end of an aisle. He let out an "Ehhhhhh."

Since I was in no mood for dialogue at this very moment, I agreeably said, "Which one, buddy?"

I received an incoherent response, so I grabbed some plastic pinwheel thingy, put it in his lap, and kept our wheels rolling. Aidan expressed his displeasure by saying, "Noooo!" I remained aloof and held steadfast in my purpose for this mission. Soon the refreshing cool air of my favorite aisle breathed our direction and I swiftly made my routine selection. I instinctively knew we were halfway home as we made our last turn to the cashier.

In the checkout line I heard behind me, "Hey, Kyle. This your son?"

I turned to see Riley's softball coach. I responded, "Hey, Coach. Good to see you. Yeah, this is Aidan."

Riley's coach looked at Aidan with a big smile and said, "Hey, pal. How old are you?"

There was a major pause. It was as if someone had asked Aidan to solve a quadratic equation. I made fixed eye contact with Aidan so that he would be focused on me and precisely repeated the coach's question word by word: "Aidan. How old are you?"

There was a brief pause. Then Aidan held up four bent fingers and said, "Fah."

The coach gave Aidan an "Attaboy," followed by an UNreturned high five *(Dad couldn't help but grimace hard at that one.)*, and we bade our adieus.

While Aidan's expressive and communicative limitations emerged, we also became anxious about his shortage of receptive skills. Aidan had an extremely difficult time understanding simple questions. Soon after he missed his mark at the grocery store, we learned how much of a problem comprehension was going be when Aidan started group swim lessons.

We felt fairly comfortable signing Aidan up for lessons at the parks and rec department. It was mainly for some additional experience, as he could dog-paddle well enough in our own pool. As it turned out, however, Lori and I were the ones doing the learning. We were usually good about informing any teacher or instructor that

Aidan's comprehension skills were on the low side and that he might not understand directions. But when we forgot to debrief a substitute swim instructor about Aidan's situation, we discovered the depth of his receptive deficits. After the instructor, Karen, explained how to take turns, a process that usually went over Aidan's head, his group mates anxiously hand-patted the water. Aidan adapted well to the fun and did the same. When Karen motioned for Aidan, he happily waded out to her. However, what followed made me take some deep breaths as a woeful dad.

Karen held Aidan under his arms in a floating position and began telling him what to do next. I watched intently as Karen clearly expressed what she'd like him to do, only to be returned with a blank stare. Then I saw her correctively mouth the process in a different way, between puzzled eyebrow raises. This went on for the three activities Aidan had to do. Karen was as good as she could be with Aidan; she managed to finish the tasks feebly by providing some animated movements for what he should do. As I would do many a time in future years, I unconsciously got out of my chair, made my way over, and offered a brief synopsis of what Karen was facing with Aidan. She nodded compliantly, and Aidan completed the twenty-minute lesson unscathed. Yet this occurrence, compounded by others, made it profoundly clear that Aidan also needed more help than what he was currently receiving in the realm of comprehension.

It was true that Aidan's speech therapy was helping. But as he progressed, we noticed something more telling:

the more often he went, the more he improved. That may sound totally obvious, but some special-needs children respond to a fixed amount of therapy and then need only a simple maintenance plan. We were still discovering that Aidan needed all the formal therapy he could get.

We also made an alarming realization in the world of speech therapy: the type of therapy that Aidan was receiving at school wasn't nearly as effective as the exemplary forty-five-minute sessions he had experienced with Sheila. So, here's the deal with school speech therapy compared to private-practice therapy: it's discouraging.

Once Aidan turned three, Alta no longer covered his private-practice speech therapy, and we had to petition our health insurance provider to cover a portion of the speech and language services. In the meantime, Aidan became the product of a public school speech program. That's when we found out about the cold, hard truth that twenty-minute sessions of school speech do not hold a candle to the excellence of private practice. I, for one, do *not* blame the school speech teachers. They are qualified and professional. Rather, it's the system that should be on trial. The speech teachers are overwhelmed with their caseloads and given minimal contact time to manage each child's individual goals effectively. In other words, they are set up to fail. There's just not enough funding in most school systems to provide kids with a rigorous program. Aidan's school sessions are certainly better than nothing at all, but we have been forced to venture outside the school system to get Aidan the services he desperately needs.

I am a proud proponent of a quality speech program for any child who has a speech and language disability. As a coach, I have formed an athletic analogy for why speech is so important: When a player on my basketball team lacks specific fundamentals in shooting, I can teach the basics to my team as a whole at the beginning of practice for fifteen minutes and hope he picks it up. Then I'm pressed to move on to our passing, dribbling, offensive, and defensive drills. Unfortunately, the player who really needs help with shooting loses. He's not going to improve much with the team-teaching approach alone. He needs me to work with him one-on-one for a significant amount of time so that we can break down each facet of his shot and refine his mechanics. Then we need to reinforce my instruction over and over until he gets it. So it is with the child who struggles with the fundamentals of speech and language: allow ample individual time to assess the areas of need, and then provide the necessary practice strategies to enable success.

13: ABA: Calling All Robots

AT THE AGE of four, Aidan qualified for applied behavior analysis (ABA) through Alta, and he received twenty hours per week of one-on-one tutoring. Next to speech therapy, this has by far been the most beneficial treatment to Aidan's development.

ABA is an in-home therapy tailored to your child's specific strengths and needs. It primarily targets kids with autism but also addresses other autistic spectrum disorders (Asperger's syndrome, PDD-NOS [pervasive development disorder—not otherwise specified], and Rett syndrome), anxiety disorders, and poor self-care skills. The individualized instruction can range anywhere from four hours to forty hours per week. Based on a thorough evaluation, the ABA provider devises a plan, and a trained tutor works with your child on one or more of the following skills:

- receptive and expressive language
- living skills
- social skills
- engagement and attention
- fine and gross motor skills
- cognitive skills

In addition, parents are trained to teach these vital skills.

Let me begin by explaining the cast of characters involved in this vital treatment program. Two young women (tutors) were assigned to work with Aidan every weekday (lucky guy!). One gal, named Miss Sue, had two years of experience working with special-needs kids and was studying for her master's degree in child development. She was fairly impressive. Miss Lorna, on the other hand, was an art history major who needed a job—any job. She did mention that her nephew had autism, so that must make her qualified . . . right?

These two tutors reported to a lead tutor (who would sometimes work with Aidan), who reported to a consultant (who would occasionally drop by to observe Aidan), who reported to a supervisor (who vaguely knew Aidan from a quarterly report she received). I viewed it as standard military protocol, meaning that someone always seemed to be getting orders from a superior, who needed further documentation on what was being performed. All the while, the person (tutor) closest to the action had the best ideas about what should be implemented but lacked the status to make an executive decision. I appreciated the method in practice but was mystified by the potential red tape of it all.

ABA initiated itself this way for Aidan:

For the first ten days, the tutors simply played with him to develop a rapport.

Next, lessons were gradually introduced until it the sessions consisted of totally instruction-based learning.

Quarterly, new and challenging lessons were initiated, while other lessons not yet mastered would continue.

And on it would go until the provider believed Aidan had reached his potential, or until the parents decided they'd had enough of the in-home invasion.

To kick-start Aidan's ABA voyage, his tutors introduced an excellent communicative tool: the picture board. The tutors made laminated cards with pictures of things like table time, break time, sensory, and puzzles. Little Velcro tabs were placed on the back of the cards so they could be moved around at will. While some of these icons were intended to help Aidan verbalize his needs, such as a glass of water or a trip to the bathroom, Aidan did have some vocabulary by then, so he mainly used the picture board as a guide to his daily events. This was good stuff, because moving from one activity to the next was Aidan's biggest hurdle. Frustrating battles inevitably occurred when we shifted Aidan from one casual lesson to another. For example, when he was practicing how to say when his birthday was, and then we drastically changed gears by having him name objects around the house, he opened up a can of temper tantrums akin to a hungry baby being denied access to her mother's breast milk. Therefore, we were thankful to the preparatory picture board for helping ease the transitional pain that we all seemed to experience.

After a year of being drilled with scripted questions associated with scripted answers, followed by even more rote phrases and mechanical responses, Aidan had had enough of being a robotic parrot. His temper flared up more often at school, and his outbursts became longer in duration. We felt lucky that Aidan's tantrums usually lasted less than five minutes, as compared to horror stories we'd heard about other kids going into two-hour frenzies. Even so, we knew these meltdowns did not represent our son's true self.

Yet the lessons and concrete work that ABA provided were definitely noteworthy. Aidan had come a long way in the first two years, but he had stopped responding to the current teaching approach. During ABA, however, he became potty trained (at least during the day), developed a comprehension of "first-then" statements, and mastered some key self-help skills, such as brushing teeth, washing hands, and getting dressed. But by the age of six, it was evident that the learning was waning and the problematic behaviors were increasing.

So, Aidan's ABA supervisor (his third since beginning the program) said, "Aidan is noticeably a fun-loving child who craves physical play. Let's move him to a play-therapy method. While engaging him in a game like shooting baskets, playing catch, or connecting train tracks, we'll create the lessons and questions around that. We'll also move to a more real and social approach to his learning."

This seemed too good to be true, but it worked! Aidan's disposition relaxed. He was more open and accepting, and his inflamed stubbornness subsided. Don't get me wrong—he still had his moments, but he thrived with this new and improved way of learning. He has been doing this type of ABA therapy now for the last two years (ages six to seven) and is a much happier kid because of it. Aidan has made strides in applying appropriate social skills, such as greetings and taking turns. His outbursts have decreased considerably, and he has learned to follow specific instructions.

However, while Aidan certainly loves structure, burning the candle at both ends has taken its toll. Hopping, skipping, and jumping from speech therapy to OT to ABA has been arduous. By the end of each week, the whole family has been getting gradually but progressively burned out trying to maintain all these formal learning environments.

Lori and I have had to do some massive soul-searching in this area. We have come to realize that while we want to improve and enhance our children's lives in any way possible, they still need unstructured time to express their innate wants and desires. We need to allow them to play for the sake of playing. We feel that giving our kids unstructured downtime has been critical for their self-worth. I like to call it decompression. It's what I need to do after a long day toiling at the grindstone. Just as I kick my feet up to watch the ball game (Go S.F. Giants!), read my favorite health magazine, or surf the Internet to calm my emotional waves, our kids need that kind of release too.

In spite of being a little overextended, Aidan has progressed nicely with ABA therapy. Recently we began to phase it out. Eventually the ABA hours will be decreased to the point where Lori and I will become the sole providers of new behavioral strategies for Aidan. We already know we'll be fairly comfortable when it's time to cut the proverbial umbilical cord, as we have been intricately involved in Aidan's lessons throughout his program.

The hard truth is that it's tough work—especially if you're doing it right! ABA tutors are trained professionals who have painstakingly sat, run, jumped, and played with Aidan for hours at a time, all with the patience of a loving grandparent. This is exhausting to do with any little boy, but especially with a potentially stubborn and inflexible special-needs child like Aidan. So when that crutch is gone and Lori and I are placed at the forefront, we will have no choice but to carry the torch forward. I'd like to believe that we'll make the transition smoothly, but I don't think our sanity is at the same level as our ABA tutors. We'll miss these adored saints. Nevertheless, it will be nice to have our home to ourselves again.

To sum up my thoughts on ABA: The revolving door of tutors spun wildly over the course of Aidan's ABA program. Take Miss Lorna, one of Aidan's first tutors. She plainly wasn't a good match for Aidan, so we requested a change with Aidan's supervisor. Our instincts proved correct, as she quit being a tutor a month later.

This early event in the program was a learning moment for us. Lori and I initially weren't particularly bold in communicating Aidan's needs with the person in charge of providing his therapy. We felt so fortunate to have the service that we merely listened and accepted the professional's advice. But when we took action by requesting that Miss Lorna take a permanent tour of the Metropolitan Museum of Art, it proved to us that we did have some control over who would bestow treatment upon our boy.

And ABA surely isn't for every family. During therapy sessions there was definitely a burden upon our family and our house. Riley didn't always understand why all this attention was being directed toward her brother or why she had to be quiet or go to another area simply because the tutors were there.

One parent told me that she tried ABA, but her family of six just could not sustain it. I felt bad for both parents because their two autistic children and one nonverbal child could have benefited significantly from an ABA program.

14: Playgroup: Yes, This Is Therapy

CAN'T A KID just *play*? I mean, can't you just roll out a ball or point to the swing set in the distant playground and let him have at it? Sure, I guess you could. But what if you want your child to "just play" with another child? What if you want to invite the neighborhood kid to join you and yours at the park to make a sand castle or to build a cool fort or something?

Oh, how I wished I could just *do* that. But the truth is that most kids on the autistic spectrum lack that natural social skill to engage in appropriate social play—and Aidan fit the mold. That's where playgroup made its needed entrance into our lives.

Aidan, four years old at this point in his autistic career, received (through Alta—thanks again, Alta!) a service called playgroup therapy. The company that provided us with this valuable resource was called MAPS (Montessori Autism Programs and Services).

What we liked about MAPS was that they facilitated Aidan's play with neurotypical peers called expert players (I refer to them as gentle souls). And facilitating these dynamic interactions were two trained adults called play guides. How they engaged and managed Aidan and his eclectic group of five was nothing short of amazing. These energetic gals in their early twenties catered to Aidan's social quirks and deficits with tireless patience twice a week for an hour and a half at a time. I'm exhausted just thinking about it.

It wasn't smooth sailing to start, though. Aidan began the program not wanting to walk down the long and narrow concrete path leading to the door of the Fun Room (as I like to call it). While he begrudgingly allowed me to turn the doorknob, I'd have to gingerly coax, then outright shove, him inside. We saw humungous Legos, wooden train sets, colorful beanbags, hundreds of marbles, a box of dress-up clothes, and many more entertaining objects. What was not to like?

Aidan was completely disinterested, but after a couple weeks of his usual stubborn transitional processes, he finally came around. Maybe it was the water balloon toss that was happening when I picked him up on a sunny day, or the organized game of tag that had the group giggling around a tree, or the boundless tolerance of the play guides. I'm not sure. All I know is that he now loves going to MAPS.

It was also evident after those first few weeks that the staff was honing in on some key social-development strategies for Aidan. In one instance, the lead play guide shared with me that they had been working on helping Aidan to share the trains and to communicate with a child who might want one. (It was no surprise to me that Aidan needed assistance in this area, since he hoarded trains territorially at home.) I was glad to hear he was making progress in this area, because Aidan seems to think that any toy he comes in contact with becomes his until eternity.

Several months into the program, I could describe Aidan's progress, in baseball terms, as a solid base hit. Once, on our way to playgroup, I asked, "Are you going to have fun at playgroup today?"

Aidan responded, "Cole, chase."

I immediately inferred that he wanted to play tag with a boy from his class. At this point in Aidan's social development (he was seven years old at the time), he rarely brought up any names of his classmates, let alone an activity that he wanted to do with a peer. Aidan's play guide confirmed that Aidan and Cole had been seeking each other out to play interactively rather than just engaging in parallel play. Lori and I couldn't have been more thrilled with this news, and it only got better.

However, we still hit certain snags in Aidan's development, and we had to address the issues and practice appropriate behavior at home. For example, his desire to enter his first semi-organized game of dodgeball at Sky High, our local trampoline center, brought on new challenges.

When Aidan entered the ring of fire, as I like to call this chaotic game, the teams were haphazardly throwing dodgeballs back and forth. Aidan was being pelted—thankfully not in the face—as he reached down for the nearest ball. He stood up and seemed to survey the war-torn city like a general. Then, with uncanny decisiveness, Aidan wound up and hurled his ball with perfect accuracy, and it landed between another boy's shoulder blades. Unfortunately, the boy was only two feet away—and on Aidan's own team.

The kid turned around and looked at Aidan as if to say, "What the heck, dude?!" Aidan offered a detached response and continued his friendly fire among his comrades. Finally, the high school employee in charge told Aidan he was out of the game, since Aidan had been hit countless times. Aidan fell to the ground in frustration.

Rest assured, Dad organized a family backyard game of dodgeball the next day. We used the commonsense skills we'd learned from MAPS. The game followed two clear rules: (1) throw the ball only at your opponent (clearly defined and discussed before the game), and (2) no meltdowns when you have to leave the game after being hit by the ball (we acted out the appropriate way to leave the game ahead of time). After fifteen minutes of many hard-fought battles, Kira ended up claiming the most victories—she is the most competitive family member—but I believe Aidan and I had the most fun.

By the end of Aidan's four-year participation in MAPS he developed social skills that constitute a home run in my score book. The proof of his progress was how he applied these skills at school. For example, according to the employee on yard duty, Aidan was able to respond appropriately to classmates at recess when they asked him to play kickball. Aidan was also able to ask students to play on the bars with him. The challenging part was when they said no; this occasionally set off a turbulent display of disappointment followed by a brief cooldown period. Still, Aidan has shown further improvement in this area and has been able to build genuine, positive relationships.

Lori and I were grateful to close our tenure with MAPS at a graduation ceremony. Our proud little boy stood there in his cap and gown with his even prouder parents looking on.

15: My Gym: A Place Where Authentic Special-Needs Therapy Can Come True

IF YOU WANT to find out if your child is coordinated, has social skills, and can comprehensively carry out instructions, this place is for you.

My Gym is a small, child-centered facility that works with any child from ages six weeks through thirteen years. Whether your child is neurotypical or has special needs, they'll take 'em. They have one-hour, weekly classes that incorporate music, dance, relays, special rides, gymnastics, sports, and more. There are three to twelve children per class, with a typical student-teacher ratio of six to one, depending on the ages of the kids.

Knowing what you know about Aidan, you can already guess the hardships that he (we) had to endure in the beginning phases of this life-skills educational course.

Early on, our four-year-old was noncompliant to most directions given by the My Gym instructors. He would often fall to the ground in defiance and scream his displeasure whenever it was time to change activities. We had to be constantly on the alert when observing Aidan from behind the counter. This would ultimately lead to our pulling him from the group for a time-out. I'd like to say I got used the other parents' stares and grumblings within earshot, but who can truly get used to that? I learned to just grin and bear it and focus on the job at hand, which was supporting Aidan.

Fortunately, Aidan had a positive role model teaching his class. Mr. Kyle was by far the most inspiring, enthusiastic, and motivating young man I have ever met. How he managed to bring his A game every week to wrangle these ten hyperactive jumping beans is beyond me. This guy performed his Vegas-like entertainment act at least six times a day, five days a week! His patience and compassion working with the kids' diverse personalities made him wise beyond his years. The type of child didn't matter; Mr. Kyle had them all actively engaged. They were movin' and groovin' to whatever wall-climbing, foot-hopping, bar-hanging activity he had them involved in. Mr. Kyle was the Pied Piper of the My Gym experience, and those eager little mice would follow him anywhere.

These children were not only learning how to follow directions, but also gaining confidence in tackling their innermost fears. For example, My Gym had a mini zip-line cord in its carnival-like room of fun. One instructor would turn on the *Mission: Impossible* theme music, and the kids would quickly line up near Mr. Kyle, who would then safely guide them to a platform of high anxiety. (Actually, it's only six feet high.)

By the time Aidan reached the front of the line, he was mesmerized by the shrieks of delight the children before him exhibited as they flew twenty-five feet through the air, all the while hanging in death-grip fashion from a wooden bar.

The other instructor completed the excursion by skimming the lone bar back along the zip line to Mr. Kyle's grasp. Then Mr. Kyle would hold the bar of flight in one hand, while the other hand effortlessly hoisted my apprehensive son. From my vantage point, I witnessed Aidan instinctively grab hold of that rod of speed. This was followed by an instinctive "No-thank-you" shake of the head from Aidan, but an encouraging nod of "Yes-thank-you" from me toward the instructor. And off he soared down the runway.

If Aidan's eyes alone could tell a story, it would have been one of horror, intrigue, delight, and joyful endings. Upon his arrival at the open arms of the waiting instructor, he couldn't remove himself fast enough to get in line again. He was hooked! With one wild three-second ride, Aidan overcame adversity, built his courage, and, most important, had fun.

The only unfortunate aspect of that session was Aidan's meltdown when the activity was over. But that paled in comparison to the confidence he built with every My Gym session he attended over that two-year span. Lori and I felt Aidan gained so many life-skill attributes through the "Mr. Kyle experience" that we enrolled all of our children in this weekly endeavor.

16: Relative Support: The Good, the Bad, and the Indifferent

I'M GOING TO cut to the chase here: raising Aidan, in regards to his autism, has been no picnic. And we realize we simply cannot expect our relatives to truly empathize with what we are experiencing. That being said, we are lucky. We are blessed to have supportive brothers and sisters-in-law who do care about and attempt to understand our situation. We are also fortunate that their children, "the cousins," are genuinely accepting of Aidan. They don't shy away from his oddities or frustrations, nor do they avoid him. Sure, they have their questions about why he does what he does sometimes, but their overall behavior is a testament to the noble job their parents are doing in raising them as tolerant individuals.

Inconveniently for them though, they do get thrust into our autistic life on occasion. Case in point: Each summer, Lori's side of the family packs up and heads to Lake Tahoe, California. We cram all sixteen family members into a rented log cabin for a lovely week of getting to know each other better. The intentions behind the family trip are good. There's a pizza night, an ice cream night, and a board game night for all the kids. We go to the beach every other day, with pool days in between. The itinerary is sublime for any family of neurotypicals. Did I say *neurotypical*? I meant *normal*. (A brief interlude as I get on my soapbox: I'm aware that my choice of words—*neurotypical, normal*—might rub some people the wrong way. But I refuse to sugarcoat this issue. Autism is *not* normal. It's a disorder. Attempting to create a facade around the truth of autism is, in my view, pure fantasy, neglect, and denial. All families certainly have their struggles. I get it. But most folks inherently start from a "normal" foundation. After that, I figure it's their choices (and the choices of their children) that make life harder or easier. Most people, however, aren't dumped headfirst into a lifestyle that presents complexities at every turn.)

The cousins range in age from four to eighteen. Of the eight kids who go to Lake Tahoe each summer, ours are the three youngest. Lori and I spend our time keeping our little angels as constructively busy as possible, especially Aidan.

With all the therapy Aidan has received over the years, he has become programmed to crave the structure of it. And while we want him to be "just a kid," we know that we have to continue with certain aspects of his therapy and day-to-day development no matter where we are or what we're doing.

So, in the spirit of learning and development, there I am playing trains with four-year-old Aidan on the rustic floor of the cabin, all the while applying my play therapy techniques and ABA strategies. I later throw on his listening-therapy headphones because I notice him getting agitated in the new environment. This grounds him some, and soon a compassionate cousin elects to play the board game Candy Land with Aidan. This provides me with a much-needed break and gives Aidan a chance to work on his social skills with someone near his age level. Ten minutes into their game, Aidan has a meltdown because he's not getting his desired picture cards—just the color cards are appearing. Aidan doesn't care about winning or even finishing the game; he just wants to flip over a candy picture card. This must be a ton of fun for his opponent, huh?

Lori comes to the rescue and ends up removing Aidan from the area (despite many sincere attempts at specific, constructive intervention methods). She successfully switches him to an independent activity, and soon it's lunchtime. One of Aidan's helpful aunts signs up for the job to sit with him while he eats a perfectly cut hot dog and some strawberries. But alas, the strawberries weren't sliced the way he usually receives them, and they weren't presented to him on his usual blue plate. So naturally, Aidan makes it perfectly clear to everyone in attendance how he feels about lunch: a fervent scowl, followed by a loud grunt of displeasure, and finally a jolting shove of the food away from his reach.

And so the week progresses, as the other adults relax in their lounge chairs on the beach, and Lori and I tend to the frustrations and nuances of helping Aidan play in the sand.

Did I mention that Grandma and Grandpa (Lori's parents) are on this family excursion? Thank goodness for that, because they are our saviors at the beach. Grandma, in particular, has a knack for swooping up Aidan and taking him for a walk when he becomes distressed. Then, moments later, he's happily eating his licorice in the shade next to his grandma.

I don't know what it is with grandparents, but they seem to see the whole picture when it comes to raising kids. While Lori's parents live in Arizona, they still visit and support us whenever they can. It's clear that they love their grandchildren, and I know they have a special place in their hearts for Aidan.

Our brothers and sisters-in-law can sympathize from afar, but our parents come the closest to understanding our issues. I think they see the big picture due to dealing with the trials and tribulations of raising their own children to full circle—that is, seeing their own kids have children. So, while they don't necessarily have the remedies for what we're experiencing, they can appreciate the challenges we're facing and they use their abundant life experience to help out in whatever way they can.

It's not that the other family members don't care. They do. They and their children simply have their own scope of issues that are just as big of a deal to them as our concerns about Aidan are to us. I guess it's all relative (no pun intended).

For example, when a family member stresses out about his kid getting snubbed at a friend's party, or his child not receiving enough playing time on a sports team, we are bummed for them. But it is difficult for us to feel too distraught when we look over our shoulder and find our own mountainous issues looming.

The *good* is that they all generally care and support us when they can.

The *bad* is that our situation has resulted in a feeling of isolation. Lori has not received the typical periodic invitations to some family gatherings on her side of the family. Maybe it's because they figure she won't be able to make it, or perhaps they think our situation will be burdensome to the group. Either way, I know Lori would appreciate the invitations.

The *indifferent* is that our relatives have their own families and challenges to tend to. Therefore, there is an inherent disconnect between our circumstances and their own daily ordeals. However, Lori and I completely understand.

17: Our Respite Quarterback

SOME TIME AGO, Lori and I realized that we had not had a Date Night for about three years. Our children were six, four (Aidan), and two, and while we were happy to have loving grandparents provide us a quick getaway for a bite to eat, we really hadn't had a full evening out to get to know each other lately.

This topic came up in one of Lori's special needs mommy groups when another mother mentioned the concept of respite. She said that because of her special-needs child, she found it difficult to ask friends or even relatives to watch her kids so she could have time to get the groceries, let alone enjoy a night out with her husband. She explained that respite care is a short-term type of care that helps a family take a break from the daily routine and stress of raising children with disabilities.

Lori came home and relayed this wonderful news. "Sign me up!" I said eagerly, and soon I was instructed to attend a mandatory two-hour training course twenty miles away from our home.

Upon entering the training room (an elementary school's staff meeting room) I found a capacity crowd of parents and guardians of special-needs children. I signed in at the first table I saw and grabbed an informational pamphlet. The buzz of the assembly told me that there was a wide range of cultures, ages, and eclectic personalities. It was just more reinforcement to my thinking that autism is indeed borderless—and that this disorder is a growing trend that affects more people than I realize.

I robotically shuffled my way to the next table and grabbed some watered-down coffee and a complimentary mini muffin. I hunched my way to an open seat and exchanged a clueless smile with a fellow naive parent beside me. Soon the PowerPoint presentation began. There were colorful charts, tables, graphs, and pictures. There was also a list of frequently asked questions and fundamental points that every parent or caregiver should know. I was so impressed with our host and the surplus of useful information she offered that I couldn't think of a single question when she completed her outline of Respite 101. And with the cessation of only one line of questioning by a dubious man in the front row, we were herded to the back of the room to sign some paperwork . . . and soon were ceremoniously dubbed "respite vendored parents." As I strolled out the door I felt well versed about the ins and outs of respite care and was ready to go—or so I thought.

Two weeks removed from my respite class, Lori and I got our act together and arranged for a respite worker (sitter) to come to our home to watch our three children. Since the sitter had been screened through a formal interview with United Cerebral Palsy (UCP) to get the job, we assumed she had some training or expertise in dealing with special-needs children.

Well, call us fuddy-duddies or say we're old-fashioned, but our mouths dropped open when we met Zoey, our first respite sitter. I'm kind of a first-impression guy, so when I shook hands with this twenty-three-year-old woman, who looked a haggard thirty-three, I was keenly aware of the bold and colorful tattoos on her forearms and calves. I quickly retracted my prejudiced thought and said to myself, *Hey, Kyle, lighten up. Zoey's probably a fantastic individual who wants to make a few bucks helping families of special-needs kids.* So I engaged her in conversation.

Here's what I learned: After dropping out of high school, Zoey made the mistake of marrying the wrong guy. But her current, out-of-work boyfriend was a "cool dude" who really understood her needs and was helpful in caring for her six-year-old son. She wanted to work full-time, but she often got lazy after a week of doing the same thing.

Whoa! You can learn a lot about someone in five minutes.

Lori and I ended up skipping our movie plans. Instead we decided to enjoy a meaningful and romantic Starbucks coffee together before hightailing it back home. Just twenty minutes after heading out the door, we were back, explaining that Lori wasn't feeling that well and we were home to stay for the night.

Now, I'm not saying we were ready to trade our quarterback, but we were going to give the backup a try.

Enter Rachel, a nineteen-year-old college student who lacked any noticeable skin decorations. On our next attempted Date Night, Rachel arrived and I gave her my let's-engage-in-conversation screening test. We chatted for about ten minutes, and I discovered that she was attending the local junior college and was considering being a special education teacher someday. Also, her nephew was autistic and she regularly took him to the park on weekends.

Okay! Now we've got someone who can throw a pass down the middle of the field!

That evening Lori and I dined at our favorite sushi place from yesteryear. I savored my cooked fish and large cold brew while she chewed on some tentacles that didn't interest me much. We felt fairly comfortable, but we still couldn't find it in our hearts to leave our kids with a stranger long enough to take in both dinner and a movie in one night. So we demolished the last of the edamame and headed for home.

Rachel and our kids seemed content enough. Aidan was playing trains, Riley was listening to music in her room, and Kira was drawing at the kitchen table. Rachel was on the couch reading her magazine, exactly where she was when we left. We graciously thanked her, gave her some extra funds for her troubles, and sent her on her merry way.

When the door closed, we quickly debriefed the Rachel experience with Riley.

"Did she play with you?"

"Did she make any phone calls?"

"Did you have fun?"

Riley dully responded, "I don't know."

Lori said, "What do you mean, honey? Did Rachel play a game or do anything fun with you guys?"

Riley shrugged her shoulders and said, "Not really. She just sat on the couch the whole time and read herself a story."

It was clear to us that respite care was not all it was made out to be. The workers were not required to engage with the children or to do anything beyond making sure they didn't hurt themselves. I'm sure that if you got the right respite worker, you'd hang on to her like a dear friend. Regrettably, at the time, that was not our experience.

Months after giving up on respite care, however, we decided to revisit the program and interviewed two more potential starters (sitters). And wouldn't you know it? One of them turned out to be my former student, and she was studying to be a physical education teacher for special-needs students. I remembered her to be responsible and thoughtful, and it was evident that she had stayed that way. We feel very fortunate to have found this special young woman, who has turned out to be a perfect fit for our family. We accordingly took her as our number one draft pick and added her to our winning team.

18: DAN Doctor: Enter the Modern-Day Witch Doctor

WHEN AIDAN WAS four and a half years old and officially two years into his autism diagnosis, Lori and I still felt new to the game and were still grasping at anything that could potentially jump-start his development. While searching online we were thrilled to stumble upon something called a Defeat Autism Now (DAN) doctor. We immediately wrote ourselves an imaginary prescription for this service.

This is incredible! I thought. *Why haven't we heard of this before? I bet every parent of an autistic child is dialed in with a personal DAN doctor!*

Lori broached the subject at one of Aidan's autistic spectrum playgroup gatherings the following Sunday, as the kids kicked a soccer ball from one grassy area to another. "I guess you've heard of a DAN doctor," Lori casually said to one of the moms she had come to trust. "Do you have someone nearby you go to?"

The mother raised her eyebrows and replied, "What's a DAN doctor?"

Lori later told me she was floored that the mother had no clue what a DAN doctor was. We always felt we were the last to know.

Another mom overheard the conversation and said that she'd heard of DAN doctors and that they were kind of a controversial topic. She delicately explained that only one child in their Sunday group had been seeing a DAN doctor and that the mother was having some misgivings about what the therapy was doing to her child. She was also concerned about the cost involved.

I asked Lori to squeeze the mother for additional inside information, since our DAN doctor appointment was creeping closer by the day, but she wasn't keen on the idea.

"I just feel uncomfortable prying into the mom's DAN doctor experience, and I'm starting to feel a bit leery about taking Aidan to something that could potentially harm him."

"Harm our child?!" I wailed defensively. "What are you saying? I'd never expose my son to anything that could hurt him. I just want to give him a chance to *conquer* this autistic thing."

There was an awkward pause. I repeated the word *conquer* in my head. Questions rapidly danced through my mind: Have I not truly accepted that there is no cure? Have I not been honest with myself about Aidan's condition? Deep within my soul, am I gripping on to the hidden hope that my son will be miraculously transformed? Despite my inner struggle and self-inflicted torment, I held strong and prideful in Lori's presence.

Lori faintly shook her head and took a deep breath. I caught a grimace on her face as she marched back to the computer to research even more.

We didn't share our feelings much on the subject again until we started our two-hour journey to the Bay Area for our appointment. We stuck a LeapFrog Leapster (an electronic game device) in Aidan's hand and began our trek to what I felt was the Last Clinic of Hope and Desperation.

Lori made it clear that we were just getting some preliminary information and a *possible* evaluation by this doctor. She didn't want to commit to anything or plunge into it too quickly. I told her I was fine with that, but I also firmly reiterated that I wasn't ruling anything out. I was keeping all options on the table.

We waited fifteen long minutes in the lobby until a receptionist finally peered over the counter and said it would probably be another ten minutes, but we were welcome to wait in the adjoining room where Aidan could manhandle a plethora of sensory manipulatives.

Eventually Dr. Congeniality (I can't really decide what to call her—she has so many fine characteristics) arrived, layered in a white lab coat and the inviting disposition of a funeral director. She didn't seem particularly interested in Aidan until he delightedly started playing with an object that, with each squeeze of his diligent little fist, would light up and play some sing-songy sounds. Her "interest" quickly turned to annoyance as she firmly instructed us to take the toy away from him. Shrugging our shoulders, we complied and, luckily, Aidan had only a moderate outburst when we directed his attention to a quieter activity.

The doctor's behavior should have been strike one—maybe even strike two, given the cold greeting we received from the receptionist along with the twenty-five-minute delay from our scheduled appointment time. Really now. It isn't as if we strolled into her office for some antibiotics for our kid's sore throat. We were here for the all-encompassing welfare of our son, and we had the anxiety and apprehension of first-time bungee jumpers. Based on our research, we knew that many of the DAN doctors' proposed methods were a bit unorthodox, but we figured our initial experience would be somewhat warmer and more appealing than this. Certainly the doctor was aware of the anxiety parents go through, right? . . . Wrong!

Dr. Tolerance instinctively made the obvious observation by pointing out Aidan's behavior when shifting from one activity to another.

I was thinking, *Uh, yeah. I get it lady. That's why we're here. To fix the issues he has. I'm not too impressed with the irritated look you have on your face while you point out my son's apparent deficits.*

The doctor said that Aidan would need to undergo an at-home blood, urine, stool, and hair test, and we'd need to send these specimens to a clinic for analysis. She said we could also do some additional tests that very day in her treatment center. These test samples would also be sent off to another laboratory for proper evaluation.

In the meantime, the doctor laid out her every-weapon-in-the-arsenal-of-man treatment plan:

- biomedical treatment
- nutritional restrictions
- gluten-free/casein-free recipes
- supplements *(Oh, my! There are so many!)*
- detoxification/chelation
- hyperbaric oxygen therapy (HBOT)

The doctor sounded confident enough when she said she had been seeing positive results with other kids. However, in the far reaches of my mind, I thought, *These techniques have got to be highly experimental.* I knew I was fresh on these matters, but they all seemed so peculiar . . . yet intriguing. Nonetheless, the basic idea was to throw everything we had at the issue and to hope that something, or maybe a combination of somethings, would work. It was controversial and, I was also realizing, bound to be expensive.

After almost two hours of discourse with Dr. Wannabe Shaman, we took our drained brains back on the road heading home, and the Argument began.

Lori exclaimed, "I don't know if I want to subject Aidan to all this stuff!"

"If this will *help* him, we're doing it!" I retaliated.

This was the first time I put my foot down, literally and figuratively, as I sped through a busy intersection. I kept hearing the doctor's explanations of the alien treatments for Aidan's "warning signs" in my head: lack of eye contact, limited speech, repetitive behaviors, and rigidity in transitions.

Lori cried, "Well, I'm not chelating Aidan!"

I "calmly" roared back, "We don't really even know what that entails! If he's got toxins in his body, I want to get 'em out!"

After an hour of Shakespearean dialogue followed by long, festering silences, I reached for Lori's tear-drenched hand and delicately said, "It will be okay. We won't do anything to hurt our boy. I love him too."

She looked at me and squeezed my hand. *The same grasp I felt on our wedding day.* That gesture told me that we'd get through this together, for better or worse.

Once we received notice that Aidan's test results were in, we went back to meet with Dr. Prescribe-You-Potions in her magic voodoo shop. I found it extremely odd that we were introduced to another lady who evidently had the credentials of an RN (or was it a medical doctor? It sounded so professional at the time). I also thought it odd that this woman would sit (mutely, I might add) in our two-hour meeting (billed handsomely to us, of course). We were told that the new addition to our meeting was there to assist us with any technical questions regarding the test results. We later speculated that she was also there to guard against liability for what was or was not promised in the DAN doctor's recommendations for our son's treatment.

Here is just a *small* sampling of the tests—all of which seem arbitrary in retrospect—that were performed on our son:

- comprehensive blood panel (CBC)
- red blood cell elements (13 natural elements + 5 toxic elements)
- comprehensive food sensitivity test (95+ foods)
- metabolic analysis profile (45 incomprehensible tests!)
- glutathione blood level
- cysteine and serum blood levels
- gastrointestinal function profile (this one involved a stool sample, which was especially fun)
- urine analysis test

As we sat in the meeting and listened to all the test results (nothing remarkable), Lori noticed that the doctor began talking directly to me. There were very few times when she actually looked at Lori. What explained this? Did the doctor hone in on my anxiety and desire to get started on whatever she was presenting to us?

Strange comments flowed from the doctor's mouth: "Aidan is very sick."

"He has metal in his system that is affecting his brain."

"He is allergic to wheat, possibly having celiac disease."

"We need to get started on his treatment quickly."

It was determined that Aidan would have the full "starter kit" to battle his autistic symptoms. And while we could have spent a lot more on additional appointments, tests, gizmos, and concoctions, we felt that the starter kit's grand total of $5K was a sufficient investment for the initial jump start of his recovery process.

We started with the following at-home routine:

1. Meticulous daily preparations of Aidan's numerous powder and liquid supplements in little ceramic bowls.

2. Squirting a bad-tasting yellow substance (L-carnitine) in his mouth three times a day.

3. Administering a vitamin B12 shot in his tush. That's right: an injection in his buns once a day for a month.

4. Enforcing a gluten-free, casein-free, soy-free (GFCFSF) diet. This was a near-impossible feat given Aidan's food selectivity. For him it meant no "real" Goldfish crackers, no chicken nuggets, no ice cream, and no fries. For us it meant running all over town to find foods he would actually eat that had none of the tasty stuff in it. Trust me, it was horrible. I tried this diet too!

You're probably wondering, "So, what about that B12 shot? Aren't you the guy who would never give something to his kid unless he was willing to try it himself first?" Well, you can bet I gave it a go. I took a booster right in my own keister!

Actually, with Lori's assistance, the first shot didn't really didn't hurt at all. It was all the hype that got the heart pumping. But alas, we were no experts, and she must have hit more muscle than fat on practice attempt two, because the moment she stabbed my rear, I felt an electric laser of pain searing into my buttocks. I survived the event, hid my tears, and eventually felt we were proficient enough to give it a go with Aidan.

Now, to strategize. We knew that if Aidan saw the needle coming he'd flip out, so we had to sneak up on him. The plan was to have me distract him with getting dressed while Lori crept up on him like a crafty, mad, sinister scientist applying the dosage to her unsuspecting patient.

And with a brief but effective assault on Aidan's rump, Lori stabbed and plunged. It was so quick that she had time to discretely hide the menacing tool behind her back and offer Aidan a Cheshire cat smile.

At first Aidan acted mildly disturbed by the incident. He glared at us as if to say, "What the heck do you think you're doing? You think I didn't see you tiptoeing up on me like that? I know your tricks, you two." Then he gently rubbed the targeted spot while eyeballing Mommy.

I was so impressed by Lori's swiftness that I thought I'd give it a try the next evening. Unfortunately, I blew it. Badly. That night, as Aidan was putting on his jammies, he saw me coming from a mile away. I made my way toward him, but it was clear that he didn't like the strange instrument in my hand. He cunningly lunged away from me as if he was evading an alligator's jaws, but I bobbed to his weave, so he didn't get far. I hastily positioned the needle and stuck my son. It entered well above the intended target as I thrust my thumb forward to expel the tangerine-colored superjuice. Aidan let out a shriek, which, I'm sorry to say, sounded like a scared little schoolgirl, as a minuscule drop of blood escaped from his white flesh.

From then on, Aidan received his B12 shots from Mommy.

Actually, Lori came up with the idea of giving Aidan the injection an hour after he fell asleep so he couldn't see any shady family members moving stealthily in on him. So, lucky for us (and him, I guess), he never felt a thing after we made that adjustment.

A month later, however, *we* felt something. Our savings account was crying for attention, and Aidan's expected improvement had yet to materialize.

Two weeks into Aidan's treatment, Lori and I convinced ourselves that maybe he was talking more. And maybe he was more socially aware. And maybe he wasn't as sensory seeking or defensive. And maybe . . .

Well, after almost five weeks of the subtle torture we put Aidan through every day, we were *definitely* convinced that he was getting short tempered and frustrated more easily than usual. We wondered whether it was the effect of the eleven—yes, *eleven*—supplements we blended and gave him orally in a syringe throughout the day, or the regimen of other at-home medical ministrations we subjected him to. Either way, we did not find any of the adjustments to have concrete benefits for our son, so we decided to end our DAN doctor experiment.

If others out there found success with a DAN doctor, I wish sincere congratulations. But we never got to do that victory dance.

Looking back, I think this garbage we put Aidan through was modern-day witch doctor crap—herbs for this, supplements for that, heavy-metal detoxification for potential mercury poisoning, blah blah blah. And there was no way I was going to pay over $1K to stick my boy in an oxygen chamber for an hour (for ten sessions) if there wasn't any hard evidence that it worked either.

When we consulted with Aidan's pediatrician afterward, he said, "I wish you would have consulted with me before you went through all this." We showed him a copy of Aidan's test results, and he simply shook his head with discontent. Other wise parents responded, "Never heard of a DAN doctor." All of this just confirmed what we had already figured out on our own (but not before shelling out a lot of money that we didn't have): the DAN doctors' claims were simply too good to be true. I couldn't help conclude that some entrepreneurial young doctor or health professional had simply found a way to capitalize on the growing autism epidemic by preying on its desperate victims: well-intentioned parents and innocent children. I feel it's fair to say that most DAN doctors' level of expertise ranges from MD to naturopath and nutritionist. Apparently, they undergo a specialized one-day training program that gives them the title of DAN doctor or DAN practitioner.

Some of the treatments we used with Aidan *may* make your child physically healthier, but it's not going to cure or effectively treat any symptoms associated with autism.

Yet, as I've said before and will say again, I have never felt guilty about trying something that I thought could help my son. Lori and I have spent countless hours and dollars trying to give our son a better life. I never wanted to feel like there was something I should have tried but didn't and therefore lost my window of opportunity because Aidan was too old to have it work (whatever *it* was). With experience, however, we are becoming savvier with what has merit—and what is hogwash—for our son's development.

19: Knock Off That TV Talk!

AIDAN: "TUBBY TOAST, Tubby Toast."

   Daddy: "Hey, Lori, I think Aidan's talking."

   Mommy: "What's he saying?"

   Daddy: "I'm not sure. I think he's saying that he wants a tub of toast."

   Aidan was two years old at the time, and we discovered that he was neither talking to us nor engaging in pretend play. He was doing something called echolalia.

   While others use the term *echolalia*, we prefer to use the word *scripting*. Fortunately, this tendency has become a gateway to Aidan's verbal achievements.

   In the "Tubby Toast" case, Aidan was quoting a phrase used from the children's television program *Teletubbies*. The more he watched the show, the more he would script random snippets from it. Phrases like "La-la," "Bye-bye," "Uh-oh," and "Tinky Winky" were common utterances within the limited language Aidan possessed. I really learned to despise that program.

By age four, Aidan was regularly reciting lines that stuck out to him during his day. Whether the lines came from a movie, a commercial, a TV show, or a family member, we usually had a guessing game as to what the source was. Sometimes we had to go to Riley (only two years older than her brother) for the keys to Aidan's script.

For instance, when Aidan would play trains and his train track wouldn't connect to his liking, he'd exclaim, "Ahhh, Swiper, nooo swiping!"

We'd then look at Riley, and she'd casually say, "*Dora the Explorer.*"

When Aidan would get visibly upset about having to come inside for lunch, he'd say, "I don't want to go to the dentist!"

I'd then holler into the living room, where Riley was doing an art project: "Riiiileeeey!"

Riley would passively respond, "It's *Caillou*, Daddy!"

We eventually realized that Aidan was using these phrases to express how he was feeling. Expressing himself with normal talk was clearly challenging, so he found an easier way to tell us how he felt.

Some of his phrases were acceptable ("Blue skidoo, we can too!" from *Blues Clues*), and some were unacceptable ("I'm not going to talk to you anymooore" from *The Wonder Pets*). While we were partially thrilled that Aidan was jump-starting his vocabulary, we questioned how many of the words he truly understood.

When Lori and I had had enough of a particular script, we'd find a new program for Aidan to watch, but he would invariably find a new phrase to torture his sister with. One day, when Riley had had enough of the annoying conversation, she yelled at Aidan, "Knock off that TV talk!" Thus the new phrase to describe Aidan's peculiarity was born: "TV talk."

The TV talk morphed into physical reenactments as well. Aidan would get into a crouch position and pretend that he was jumping into a TV picture while reciting the "blue skiddoo" line, and he would practically act out entire episodes of *The Upside Down Show*.

With all of the TV talk and theatrical performances, you might ask, "How did you get all this to stop?"

Well, I learned that echolalia is part of the natural progression for someone learning to talk. When young children babble in a rhythmic way, they are actually mimicking language, thereby learning it. When autistic children copy sounds, words, and phrases that they hear adults use, they may be merely adapting to the language in a different way. The process may be slower and a little off the wall, but scripting represents emerging skills.

Nonetheless, we couldn't have Aidan parroting phrases constantly in his classroom or other learning environments. So, we did (and continue to do) our best in providing him a free location where he can do his scripting: his room. All over the house we have laminated signs that read NO SCRIPTING HERE! And there's one self-release sign in his room saying SCRIPTING OKAY HERE!

Now, when I call him out on his TV talk and, refer-ring to the posted sign, say, "Aidan, would you like to go script in your room?" he quickly says, "No-thank-you," as if he's embarrassed and upset that I invaded his happy place.

There are times when he's rattling off something that I can't identify—I know only that it's irritating and inap-propriate—and I bluntly say, "Aidan, no TV talk!" This makes him mad, but he stops. Some may say that I'm sti-fling his speech and language development; however, I believe I'm increasing his opportunities to grow socially and to make friends. I'm not sure this technique is work-ing, but we'll keep up the good fight.

Lori and I are constantly feeding Aidan the appropri-ate words for a given situation. We have learned to read his body language and to take action swiftly. Then we at-tempt to provide him with a phrase that will match his emotion or general demeanor. This has been a powerful tool granting Aidan an opportunity to interact properly both with his peers and with us.

When Aidan gets flustered, we find ourselves saying, "Use your words." And while he may take a few seconds searching for them, he usually puts together an utterance that we can both understand.

I am frequently saying to Aidan, "What are you script-ing?" so he knows that what he's doing is removed from social reality. After much prodding, Aidan will usually answer with the TV show or video game it came from. I hope he'll eventually come to realize that scripting is inappropriate in public settings. (I'd like him to have a date to the school dance someday, you know?)

You might be thinking that this boy has too much technology in his life, but he scripts books too. We thought Aidan was reading at an early age, only to discover that he had memorized the whole book *Put Me in the Zoo* by Robert Lopshire. He'd look at each page and simply recollect what Daddy had read the prior night. In retrospect, he must have recalled numerous parts of the Berenstain Bears, Mo Willems, and Dr. Seuss collections, too. It's impressive but eerie to think about what's going on in that brain of his. We learned that it's common for those with autism to be able to script entire children's books or movie lines. (Sorry, Aidan, you're just a *normal* autistic kid.)

Echolalia, scripting, TV talk, or whatever the hip term is at the time can be very strange to observe. Because Lori and I are all too conditioned to it, we have to take a step back sometimes and assess it as if we are seeing and hearing it for the first time. This reminds us of how odd it can appear while allowing us to redirect Aidan to use appropriate language.

The misinformed may say that Aidan is out of his tree when talking to himself like that. Others may recognize the book he is reciting and think he's a little genius. Either way, I can't wait around for the world to recognize that he has autism and to summon understanding and tolerance for my son. I've got to give him some tools and guidance for controlling or adapting this behavior.

I've come to understand that autistics think and learn differently. This is why Aidan's echolalia has been beneficial. While it may be annoying to others, it has been a valuable stage in Aidan's speech development. How parents go about facilitating that type of learning is simply a judgment call.

20: Food: Just Try It, for Goodness Sake!

"GAAAAAACK!"

"What was that?" I asked Lori from the living room.

Lori said, "It's Aidan. He's eating those veggie puffs for toddlers, and he keeps gagging on them."

Curious, I watched him having his snack and, sure enough, every few puffs . . . "GAAAAAACK!"

It didn't seem to bother Aidan, though. His eyes would water up a bit and he'd swallow deeply, but there were no worries from his perspective.

This event, back at age one, was the first indicator that Aidan had some sensory issues. There were even a few occasions when Aidan would stick his fingers down his throat while chillin' in his high chair in order to achieve this gagging sensation. Afraid he'd swallowed a quarter or something, I'd jerk my head in his direction, only to find him withdrawing his hand from his mouth with a hazy smile. Knowing what I know now, it should have raised a red flag, but we had no clue back then.

By the time Aidan hit his third birthday, it was clear he was more than finicky about his eating habits. His diet consisted of plain hot dogs, chicken nuggets, and fishy crackers. By the time he turned five, he added some chips and some sweets, but that was basically it—unless you count water and Capri Sun juice as food.

When Riley had her sixth birthday party, Aidan had just turned four. To my astonishment, he was the only kid at the party not eating ice cream—by choice! It finally sank in that he was resisting most foods.

Well, no child of mine was going to refuse God's greatest dessert gift to mankind! When we got home from Riley's party, I immediately made him a small bowl of the creamiest and most satisfying delicacy known to kids (and adults) around the globe. I sat beside him and forced a spoonful of goodness into his lock-jawed mouth. A smidgen made it through his pursed lips, while the rest dribbled down his chin.

It took him a moment to register what had happened; it was as if his brain were running on hamster-wheel power. He didn't have much language at the time, but after he had a chance to reflect on what had passed his lips, he brought his hands up a few inches from his face, touched his fingertips together twice (sign language for "more"), and promptly said, "Mmmooorrre."

Yes, Dad was the hero that day. Although I have created an ice cream–eating monster, my boy now enjoys the closing to every birthday party. He also enjoys his chocolate ice cream cones at home almost every afternoon after school.

And because Aidan didn't have enough therapies in his life, we thought we'd add food treatment to his list too.

When Aidan was five we worked with his ABA therapist to implement a food plan within his daily regimen. His tutors would spend approximately thirty minutes having him try a food that we wanted to include in his diet. Basically, each session would start by having Aidan work for a food he liked, such as a Hostess CupCake, by eating a new food. We'd always begin small—for example, with six peas. Then we'd follow up the next day with nine peas, then eleven, then thirteen. . . .

The tears and refusals sometimes lasted up to one hour. But by the fifth day, Aidan was popping peas like a teenager eating popcorn at a movie. Well, maybe not that readily, but he'd made progress.

We tried all kinds of tasty treats for kids: yogurt, almonds, green beans, cheese, chicken breast (totally different from chicken nuggets, from Aidan's perspective), and gooey peanut butter.

What bothered me most during his food therapy was the amount of patience shown to Aidan. Don't get me wrong; I liked the fact that his tutors were tolerant. But his stubbornness was just so gosh-darn acceptable to them.

After a while, I felt it was time to implement the Daddy Method of food therapy. Now, what I'm going to tell you may make you want to call child protection services, but those people don't work with autistic kids 24-7, and they don't know my kid like I do. I had to combat his stubbornness in a way that only a father would be permitted to implement under his own roof: I flat out forced him!

Over the weekend I tried my own experimental approach. The food of our (okay, my) choice today was chips. They weren't just any chips, though. These were different in shape, size, and color from the Ruffles Aidan was accustomed to.

Oh, the humanity!

When Aidan would say, "No!" and inevitably push his bowl away with a protracted whine, I used a stern testosterone-enhanced voice—not a yelling voice, but a powerful reverberation that would rock his world like a polar bear dominating a fish.

Here's a sample of what took place.

Daddy: "Let's work for a cupcake today."

Aidan: "No-thank-you."

Daddy: "You will take a bite." (I pointed to one of the two chips.)

Aidan: "Nooooo!" (With a defiant tone that most likely came from his mother's side.)

Daddy: "Do you want me to *help* you?"

Aidan: "NOOOOO!"

Daddy: "Last chance, or I will *help* you." (I motioned to the chip again and, nodding my head, made stellar eye contact with him.)

Aidan: "NOOOOOOOOOO!!!" (Screaming with a rebelliousness that most likely came from my side.)

Daddy: "Okaaayyy."

I took a chip, pried open his little lips, and forced it into his mouth—and not with the gentleness he'd experienced in the ice cream episode months earlier. "CHEW IT!" I bellowed with strength and intensity.

His lip quivered, and the tears flowed instantaneously. But he started chewing! My heartstrings began to tug relentlessly. My heart said, *That'll do for now*, but my brain asserted, *Don't give in just yet.*

And so it continued. I would persistently force and Aidan would reluctantly chew, until the chip was consumed. This seemed to go on for long time. Aidan swallowed each *slowww* bite as if he were forcing a golf ball down his gullet.

Daddy: "One more chip, Aidan. TAKE A BITE!" (As unsympathetically as I could.)

More tears, moans, and cries. (What he displayed on the outside, I was feeling on the inside.)

Aidan: *"NOOOOOOOOOOOO!!!"* (This outburst was followed by angry cries and howls.)

Was I making a breakthrough? Could I break his will? This was a pivotal moment, and I would *not* give in.

Daddy: "DO YOU WANT ME TO HELP YOU?" (Déjà vu?)

The boy knew I meant business. He hadn't had this particular type of "patience" in his face before.

Aidan: (A whimper, then cold silence.)

Then, without warning, Aidan seized the second and last chip from the bowl. He jammed it in his mouth and furiously chomped and swallowed simultaneously. A scowl formed on his brow, and he breathed heavily.

Aidan was mentally beaten, and he knew it. Dad and was in complete control.

But in reality, I look at it as if *we* won. We won because I know in my heart that it was good for him. Aidan turned a corner in his food therapy—and in other, future therapies—because of this incident. Life just got a bit easier for him and for us. It was the acceptance not of food, but of change. And I know that if he needs to tackle something of great importance to his growth, we may have to resort to Dad's method of totalitarianism, but he will succeed.

Some may find my technique a bit too bold for their tastes. Others may find it truly revolting. And some might applaud it. I certainly cannot endorse it. But I know my boy, and I knew that the waiting game option of sitting for an hour in the hope that he would take one bite of a peanut butter and jelly sandwich was not going to help him in the long (or short) run.

I believe a dad needs to intervene with what he feels is the right thing to do. It may not always be the perfect solution, but if it comes from love, the intentions have got to be good.

Aidan and I finished our intimate and emotional battle with a hug. I told him I was very proud of him and I loved him very much. And I do believe he rebounded rather quickly, because as I cleaned up the chip crumbs, his face was full of his chocolate cupcake reward.

Years have passed since Daddy's breakthrough method, and while Aidan has been more receptive to new foods (sausage, broccoli, and blueberries) and a balanced diet, he still puts chicken nuggets at the top of his want list. The day when we share a juicy cheeseburger will be another milestone.

21: Reflecting on the Signs

WHILE THERE'S NO one specific symptom that informs parents that their child may have autism, there were some distinct signs that something wasn't quite right with Aidan. Of course, hindsight is bliss, and if we knew then what we know now, we would have jumped on those tell-tale signs earlier.

As mentioned in the previous chapter, the first sign we noticed was the *gaaaaaack* sound during Aidan's first introductions to solid food as a baby. We thought he was just getting used to it—and he was—but now we know it was something more. The gag reflex eventually subsided as he got older, but the lightbulb should have started to flicker for us. The food situation morphed into "He's just a picky eater." And while many neurotypical kids are that way, his pickiness was still an indicator of an autistic trait.

Also, when Aidan began walking at fifteen months, he would sometimes walk on his toes. I didn't think much of it until a friend said, "Looks like Aidan is going to be a sprinter for the track team." (Some runners tend to use their toes more when they walk and run.) I later found out that toe walking can be a sensory behavior. I eventually concluded that Aidan craved the feeling of walking on the balls of his feet. The cool term associated with this is *proprioceptive input*. In Wilkin's terms, proprioceptive input is an attempt to provide the body with a conscious awareness of where it is in space. Lots of autistic kids have poor body awareness, and when a child positions his feet in toe-type walking positions, he is supplying himself with that needed input. This can help regulate the child's sensory system and maybe even stabilize and calm him some. This is, technically, a theory, because I've found no definitive cause of toe walking.

The OT people have had a field day with treatment ideas for this behavior. Some have their kiddies jump on trampolines (we got a small one for our family/sensory room), walk in sand (I have taken Aidan to the park regularly for this), and stomp their feet up a flight of stairs (the neighborhood school's bleachers do wonders for him).

Aidan's eye contact was also subject for concern. Prior to his official diagnosis, we told ourselves his eye contact wasn't that bad. It's not as if he wasn't aware of us when we entered the room, but he didn't exactly make good eye contact either. Whenever he was focused on a task of choice, it took quite a bit of coercion to get his attention on us.

But the biggest eyebrow raiser was his receptiveness, or lack thereof, when we called his name. This goes hand in hand with the eye contact issue. As mentioned in chapter 2, I'd call his name (which he knew by that point), but he'd totally blow me off—or at least that was what I thought he was doing.

The straw that broke the backs of Mom and Dad was the language issue. We heard from friends, teachers, and relatives that Aidan was just a late bloomer. We'd justify this with our own excuses that we, too, had been a little behind when we were younger.

In retrospect, I believe that as parents we could have been more diligent and realistic about Aidan's developmental status early on. I'm not saying we needed to go around and compare him to every child at the park, but it's now clear that Aidan was showing some significant deficits in a couple of areas. I feel that making excuses or being in denial (for whatever personal reasons one may have) can only delay the therapy a child needs and deserves. As I've said many times to Lori, "You've got to give 'em a chance to be successful." (I know she agrees, but she allows me to get on my high horse and preach once in a while.)

22: Was It Vaccines, Genetics, or...? Just One Guy's Opinion

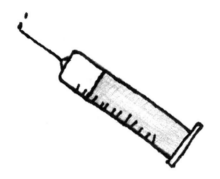

THERE ARE SOME compelling arguments on both sides of the vaccine dispute. The medical field says, "No way! Vaccines are not the cause of autism, and we have the research to prove it." Meanwhile, a plethora of parents of autistic children proclaim, "Thimerosal [which contains mercury] is the culprit!"

I really don't know for sure, but I've certainly got an opinion.

Almost two years after Aidan's diagnosis, Jenny McCarthy came out with her book *Louder Than Words: A Mother's Journey in Healing Autism*. It's a good book, but I found it didn't offer Lori and me the concrete answers we were searching for in terms of "recovering" our son.

I followed McCarthy's quest with her Green Our Vaccines march to Washington, D.C., and her appearances on CNN with Larry King. Man, is she hard-nosed! McCarthy blasted the medical professionals on the panel and made her case against specific vaccines. When one of the whipped medical puppies said that the MMR (measles, mumps, rubella) vaccine and others had saved many people from contracting illnesses, I applauded Jenny's rebuttal: "Give me mumps and measles. I'll take that way over autism any day."[2]

"You go, sweet thing!" I yelled and laughed at the TV. On CNN McCarthy also stated that her son had "recovered" from autism. There was a huge uproar about her statement in the autism community, so she clarified herself. I really liked the analogy she used:

> Let me explain that, recovered, because a lot of people get confused by that. You can't become cured from getting hit by a bus. And this is a really great analogy. But you can recover from getting hit by a bus. It's the same thing with autism. You know, these kids were mowed over. And they regained skills—their skills back through therapy. And Evan regained all those lost skills that he once had after getting hit by that bus. Now there's no cure. But you can be damn right that kid recovered. He recovered. Now I can't say cured,

---

2   McCarthy, Jenny. "CNN.com: Transcripts." Interview. CNN.com: Breaking News, U.S., World, Weather, Entertainment & Video News. 8 Apr. 2008. Web. 16 June 2011. <http://transcripts.cnn.com/TRANSCRIPTS/0804/02/lkl.01.html>.

because I don't know what he would have been like before the bus hit him.[3]

I bought that answer—for a while.

Around that time more celebrities and sports stars were coming forward with stories of autism in their families. Being a sports fan, I followed Rodney Peete's (former NFL quarterback) situation with his son. I knew at that point that autism had no boundaries. If two healthy and successful individuals had sons with autism, anyone could.

But the story that hit me the hardest was Doug Flutie's (another former NFL quarterback). Maybe it was because I knew that, at five foot nine, Flutie's making the big time was already an inspirational story to us wannabe athletes. Maybe it was because I liked his cheesy commercials with Pro Football Hall of Fame quarterback Terry Bradshaw. But when Flutie showed footage of his son laughing, talking, and making good eye contact prior to his vaccines, followed by footage of him sitting, verbally uncommunicative, in a golf cart at his home, it tore me up inside. It was clear that his boy was not fully cognizant of the world around him.

So at this point in my autism journey, I had to ask myself: do vaccinations cause autism?

Well, after Aidan's DAN doctor disaster, I'm skeptical. If vaccines cause autism, why didn't any of that glutathione (chelation), supplementation, B12 shot gibberish work for us? Wouldn't it have helped him recover just a bit from the supposed vaccine "poison"?

---

3 Ibid.

I will say this, though. The fact that American doctors recommend we give our children three times the number of vaccines as those of other countries is alarming. Is it a coincidence that the incidence of autism in the United States ranks among the highest in the world? The number of vaccines given to an American child now, versus the number given in the 1950s, is mind-boggling. Are we that scientifically advanced to presume we need all these inoculations, or is this area of the medical field simply creating more vaccines for financial gain? Furthermore, the number of vaccinations administered in a single appointment for a child is shocking. Although this is my subjective opinion, it just seems so brutal on a child's system. I remember that Aidan had a sinus infection during his vaccination period. Perhaps his tiny body wasn't at full power, and those so-called helpful poisons got to him.

One thing is for sure: we didn't take any chances with our third child, Kira. She had her vaccinations spread out over a longer period of time than Aidan did.

Were we going overboard? If you had an autistic child, you probably wouldn't take the chance either. Even if the idea of vaccines causing autism is far-fetched, we still took precautions.

Here's another thought that occurred to us: we have two neurotypical daughters, and our boy has autism. Maybe there's a connection between autism and boys! The disorder does run higher in males than in females, does it not? Well, yes. Studies have proven that correlation. However, Riley has ADD as well as a mild form of

PDD-NOS, which is actually part of the autistic spectrum. So gender doesn't tell the whole story.

Is there a genetic component, then? I must admit, there's got to be something there. Lori and I know of two families in which three of their five children are on the autistic spectrum.

This brings me to another controversial issue. Regarding the families with five children, how could the parents have had more than one kid with autism and knowingly continued to have more children?

Lori and I don't feel we have the right to call out another couple for wanting more children—that's their choice. But we definitely drew the proverbial line on more children once we detected the autism thread in our family. We do take solace in knowing that we're done with the childbirth chapter of our lives.

Moving along to another potential cause, how about complications during pregnancy? Any possibilities there?

As I mentioned in chapter 10, Lori did experience a lot of stress when she was pregnant with Aidan, mostly due to the death of her stepfather. And I always felt she needed to eat more veggies. But again, I blame no one. And I'm certainly not going to start with my wife.

Heck, my own undiagnosed ADD, as I like to call it, could have played a role. My work friends joke that I have OCD (obsessive compulsive disorder) traits, evidenced by my love of Post-it Notes and excessive focus on my email. (I just tell them, "I'm in a zone, baby!") Maybe Aidan just occupies a more magnified version of my "zone."

Also, I had a fair amount of Vicodin in my body for a foot surgery at the time Lori became pregnant with Aidan. Connection? I don't know.

More thoughts on the genetic component: To my knowledge, my family has no history of weirdness (for the lack of a sensitive term to describe autism). We're all extraverted, social creatures, and no one has ever called me shy or reserved. Yet, our kids are our kids—meaning they have many of the same traits that Lori and I have. From Aidan's and my desire for structure and routine to our similar sensitivity to the listening-therapy music, we do mirror each other somewhat. And Riley certainly displays Lori's and my ADD tendencies and subpar reading comprehension. Lori and I were more functional in school and social environments, whereas our kids are more extreme. Now if Riley could just have inherited Mommy's compulsiveness to make her bed, I'd be a little more satisfied.

Lori's family tree is also full of engineers: mechanical, chemical, electrical, you name it. The men of that family are high-level thinkers—geniuses in my book. And although they might not walk into a lively party and high-five everybody, they sure are nice guys.

I do believe in susceptibility. Maybe Lori's and my genes didn't splice as cleanly as they should have. It's possible that Aidan, being a male with "susceptible" DNA, was more prone to developing autism when he received all those vaccines.

I wish I could take a solid stance on this vaccine issue, but unfortunately I can't. I, like most in the autism community, will have to wait until further research provides a clear answer. For now, I'm undecided.

I believe the guessing game will continue for some time, but I won't be one to ponder it for too long. I'm too busy picking up Aidan and taking him to his next therapy session. Oh, and shooting baskets with him in the backyard, and wrestling on our living room floor before bedtime.

23: Special Day Class: Learning for All

FOR MORE THAN a year after the parent-teacher conference that set our journey with autism in motion, we kept Aidan in the local preschool.

Aidan was three and a half years old and was progressing well due to all the speech and occupational therapy he was receiving. He was well behind his peers developmentally, however, and had plenty of other issues that we were still discovering. It was clear at this point that, as far as labels were concerned, Aidan was a "high-functioning" autistic little boy. And it was becoming even more evident that he required a more specialized environment to meet his intricate needs. That need was a special day class.

Even though Aidan was not yet "school-aged," the local district was, according to California law, already responsible for his educational development. After a brief review of his situation, the district found it appropriate to place him in a communicatively handicapped (CH) class with a speech teacher named Linda, who spoke with a southern drawl. We were alarmed to find out that Linda hadn't set foot in a school venue for fifteen years. Apparently, she got the job based on her many years of experience teaching speech to one child at a time in a clinical environment. As guarded as we were, though, we thought positively and gave it a try.

About a month into the class, we requested a meeting with Linda. At that point in his development, we knew Aidan only had command of three-to-four-word utterances and couldn't hold conversations beyond a basic question or two. But at our meeting, Linda optimistically proclaimed, "He's doing just fine. The class is currently working on asking and answering W questions: who, what, when, where, and why."

(In retrospect, at this point Aidan was two years away from even contemplating "*What* did you do at school?" and three years from reasoning the likes of "*Why* are you sad, happy, or excited?")

After about five minutes of Linda's rubbish attempt to make us feel good, we realized she was totally clueless about where Aidan was on the learning curve. I think she figured if a kid looked at her and robotically repeated phrases along with the other students, then he was on his way to becoming a linguist. This was the wrong class—and teacher—for Aidan.

Lori and I thanked her for all of her efforts, and after we bowed and curtsied at the door, we do-si-do'ed our way to a different special day class the following week.

The new and improved special day class was taught by Miss Heather. She was enthusiastic, welcoming, and experienced in the classroom. She also had three classroom aides and lots of stimulating activities to be shared among eight eccentric and highly diverse students. The mix of the children's conditions included severe speech delay, learning disability, PDD-NOS, and autism.

At this stage we were discovering the different levels and aspects of autism. While Lori and I didn't want to go around comparing Aidan to other autistic children, it was hard not to. It helped us to understand that while Aidan was not currently on the high end of the spectrum, he certainly wasn't on the lower, or severe, end either. We found that he was able to perform enough of the life-skill tasks that allowed him to socialize with most of his peers. Socialization was one of the main things we really cared about at this time.

While I was *trying* not to make distinctions among Aidan, his classmates, and, frankly, the unnormalness, I became fascinated with the oddities and behaviors surrounding him. While all the kids had special needs, they were all so different from each other. Some appeared very happy, while others were easily agitated. I noticed that one child could not be left alone for a second, while another was free to be independent. What was largely apparent, though, was that most kids craved to be engaged in some way. They wanted to learn! Over the years, the complexity of these groups of children has affected the way I view and teach special-needs kids today. Spending time with these captivating little characters created in me an open and inviting nature. Furthermore, my appreciation for their unconventional qualities expanded my heart in more ways than I could imagine.

Our time with Miss Heather and her innovative curriculum flew by, and after a year and a half she said that there was not much more Aidan could gain from her class. In other words, it was time for him to graduate to the next level: kindergarten! Lori and I were extremely pleased with the outcome of Aidan's experience with Miss Heather and the way she fueled her students' minds with her creative lessons. Aidan learned to love school there.

Enter Ms. Anderson, her posse of classroom aides, a neighboring public school, and a new beginning.

Aidan embraced his new program, which was specifically for children on the autistic spectrum, and Ms. Anderson had these kids rockin' and rollin'. The aides were well trained for little (and big!) personas, and the kids responded favorably. Some, like Aidan, were mainstreamed based on their academic and behavioral development. Aidan was proficient enough in kindergarten math to attend that portion of teaching in the general education class. When it came to language arts, however, he stayed with Ms. Anderson and her aides for small-group instruction.

Our primary objective was to get Aidan learning in the regular-ed classroom. And to promote the goal of getting to the "other class," we were introduced to the Behavioral Data Sheet. This beneficial document was basically a daily report card to let us know how Aidan was doing.

Below is a sample data sheet that we used for Aidan. Based on his behavioral goals, it has changed each school year.

AIDAN'S DAY

ACTIVITY (Chronological Order)	Noncompliant (Refusal)	Throwing Objects	Physical Aggression	☺ On Task
Reading/Journal/ Daily Language				
Writing/Language (W+F); PE (M+T+Th)				
RECESS				
Math (M+W+F); Speech (T+Th)				
LUNCH				
RTI (T+W+Th); Music (M)				
Reading				
Social Studies/Science				

Notes to Mom and Dad: _____

Lori and I were thrilled with Aidan's updated learning environment. He grew both socially and emotionally, and we were starting to feel like we were honing in on his greatest areas of need. He did so well that we explored the idea of having him attend his neighborhood school the following year. There we hoped he would be mainstreamed in a regular-ed classroom with a one-on-one aide for the whole day.

Here is my candid and tough-talking perspective on special day classes:

I've always been puzzled by some parents' reasoning (or lack thereof) for *not* putting their special-needs children in a special day class or embracing the benefit of an aide in the regular-ed classroom. Maybe it's because they feel their children will get more out of the regular-ed environment. Perhaps they don't want any label or preconceived notion attached to their children. Or maybe they just don't want to admit, to themselves or to others, that their children need both labels and services.

Lori and I had to learn to put our egos and wistful expectations aside when it came to our son. We figured, whatever would benefit Aidan most, that's what we'd do. Who cares how he (we) may be perceived by family, friends, neighbors, or bystanders? Yes, casting aside other people's impressions is often easier said than done. I've seen Aidan stick out like a watermelon in a pumpkin patch, and I've witnessed many a raised eyebrow. But I knew I'd have to rise above all that for the benefit of my boy.

We are fortunate to have reached a point where Aidan can successfully be a part of a regular-ed class with modifications and aide support, rather than one of two harmful options: being held back in a place where his development is limited, or being placed in a regular-ed environment without an aide such that he gains nothing except the ability to say that he's in a regular-ed classroom "just like everybody else."

As parents, it is our hope that Aidan will individually go from class to class without the escort of an aide. But, for now, we're taking honest steps according to his social and academic development. I believe it will be a matter of recognizing that when our child has the ability to stand up, we need to remember to stand down.

24: Spectrum City!

THIS AUTISM THING is really a wide spectrum. Most kids are slapped with the autism label early, and while they have their generic similarities, they also have distinct differences. Even though he has a high-functioning version of autism, Aidan may share more traits with a severely autistic child displaying sensory issues than with someone in his own distinctive category. I've found that the range and level of symptoms zip all across the autism board.

Inevitably, we've become friends with other parents of special-needs children. Plight and survival had a way of bringing us together. We've gathered for barbecues and kids' birthday parties. We've talked about our children's quirks and deficits, as well as the challenges they have overcome.

On one occasion, as we observed our children playing on a backyard structure, one father said, "It's interesting.

Our kids are all on the spectrum, yet they are all so different."

He was right. His son Josh was nothing like Aidan. Josh was content to play alone and to wander from adult to adult for social interaction. Aidan preferred to chase and be chased by another boy in their custom-made version of tag. While Aidan and Josh both had their language and comprehension difficulties, they were at opposite ends of the social part of the spectrum.

The boy Aidan was playing with, Chandler, was a whiz at the English language, and he could list every street name as he navigated through our neighborhood. Aidan was obsessed with reciting house address numbers for a while, but he couldn't come close to Chandler's Copernicus-like talents.

What was clearly apparent was the social eccentricity they all possessed. None of them could pick up on social cues that would be natural to most kids. They all took things too literally and had a difficult time making reads on another person's feelings.

I believe this to be the biggest issue that autistic children face. Some may come off as aloof, rude, or ill-mannered, but that certainly isn't their intent. Most are just oblivious to certain aspects of social grace and slang terminology. Aidan had to be taught (over and over) the most natural phrases and expressions of our culture that others take for granted.

For example, each morning before school Aidan would have to pause and process my usual phrase to the kids: "Hustle up!"

Aidan would basically repeat the words "Hustle up" and do nothing. I'd immediately qualify my request by saying, "Let's go!" I soon found I needed to tell him exactly what to do: "Brush your teeth and put on your shoes." Though he's continued to hear this demand on most mornings, he hasn't quite gotten it down yet. However, I think he now knows more than he lets on about what my expression means.

To further our quest for Aidan's basic understanding of idioms and metaphors, we've initiated rudimentary knock-knock jokes. Although I'm not entirely sure he's interpreting these plays on words, I do know he enjoys laughing it up with Kira. Here's an example:

Daddy: Knock-knock.

Kira: Who's there?

Daddy: Who.

Kira and Aidan (who enjoys joining in): Who who?!

Daddy: Is there an owl in here?

Kira and Aidan: Ha ha ha!!

While the autistic spectrum encompasses many symptoms and personalities, the underlying theme is the lack of intricate social ingredients that prevent people from easily blending in: facial expressions, social cues, and cultural phrases. And that's what I feel most parents want for their children with autism: to just blend in.

25: The Advocate: Our Barracuda!

WHILE AIDAN HAD an official diagnosis of autism, our daughter Riley did not. However, with her diagnosed ADD and PDD-NOS, she was in desperate need of the services that would give her a chance to succeed in school—services that Aidan qualified for but she did not. The current support in place for Riley was noticeably not working, and something had to be done.

I share the following incredible story to shed some light on how important it is to actually have a child "labeled" in order to receive services. For without the label, one could face what we encountered with Riley. . . .

Riley's whole team was positioned at the round table:

- regular-ed classroom teacher
- occupational therapist
- speech and language pathologist
- program specialist for education

- school psychologist
- principal
- Mommy
- Daddy
- the advocate

In our bid to help Riley combat all her academic deficits and social challenges, we engaged this team in a meeting about the tools she needed to be successful in her school environment. We wanted her to have a part-time aide, which is very difficult to obtain when you don't have a label that the district deems worthy of services. At this point we were gathered for what is called, in the realm of public education, an individualized educational program (IEP). And to hedge our bet for that part-time aide (which we knew would be extremely costly for the district), we had decided to hire an advocate to support us at our meeting.

Our reasoning was that, despite my experience as a teacher, Lori and I felt a little intimidated and clueless about the rights and services associated with an IEP. That's when the idea of an advocate came into play. We knew that an advocate would draw upon her experience in representing parents' needs and desires. We trusted that she'd work assertively to attain the services to which Riley was entitled under the law.

As it turned out, advocates are pricey. The averages I've seen charge a hundred dollars per hour, and the one we went with technically wasn't even a lawyer—although she seemed to play one in person.

Our advocate, Roxanne Steele, is a powerful-looking woman standing at five feet ten inches tall, plus high heels, with long, blond hair. Her posture told us that she would never muster more than a "tee-hee" for a joke. To say she was curt or blunt could easily describe her disposition in casual situations. Her job was plain and simple: to obtain any and all services needed to support our daughter, whether the district was on board or not.

The gathering was tense from the get-go. IEPs can cause tension when parents decide to seek the assistance of an advocate. Basically, we were telling the school district that we did not fully trust that they would be forthright about the services Riley may be eligible for. Therefore, some stakeholders of the IEP likely felt defensive before we even got started.

After the standard meet and greet, Roxanne got down to business. She pulled out and efficiently started up her laptop computer, along with her handy-dandy mini tape recorder, both of which brought an added bit of tension to an already stressful situation.

The principal, sensing the impending fireworks display, initiated the proceedings and said something about how we were all there to help Riley, and he wanted to establish a basis for civility. Roxanne rolled her eyes.

Riley's second-grade teacher spoke first. She relayed that Riley was a sweet child, though she had difficulty focusing and staying on task despite the conservative interventions she had received. Thus, she said, Riley would benefit from having an aide in the regular classroom.

Riley's OT and speech teacher spoke next. She basically said that Riley was improving on the majority of her goals each month. Therefore, it was her recommendation that Riley continue with the same amount of services she was currently receiving.

Roxanne feverishly typed away on her laptop.

Then the school's psychologist, who held most of the cards to Riley's fate, had her turn. When she passed out her evaluation and recommendation, Roxanne suddenly stopped typing, pointed the cassette recorder in the elderly lady's direction, and sat upright in her seat like a lioness ready to pounce on her prey.

The psychologist was calm and confident in her delivery. She stated that Riley qualified for services, but it was based on her having multiple learning disabilities. What this meant was that Riley would receive certain supports based on her learning deficits, but she would miss out on certain vital services because her PDD-NOS was not recognized as autism. In other words, Riley would receive no aide and no support for her lack of social skills (both of which we felt were paramount for Riley to thrive in her early educational development).

No more than one minute into the psychologist's spiel, Roxanne was challenging her findings based on her choice of words, as well as her written report. Roxanne said, "Your requirement for services under ed code says not limited to on this form, and you have listed a fraction of Riley's deficits as it relates to autism." What Roxanne was eloquently and vehemently pointing out was that

Riley displays plenty of autistic behaviors not recorded on the psychologist's report, and these behaviors would easily make her eligible to receive the services we wanted.

Roxanne neither wavered nor stuttered. By attacking the psychologist's assessment of Riley and the criteria of the form she used, Roxanne quickly blasted her integrity.

"You are doing a disservice to these parents," Roxanne stated firmly.

As the frail psychologist, who had spent her career offering moral support (some may say false assistance) to the disillusioned and uninformed parent, shrank further into her chair, the principal intervened: "We cannot continue this aggressive line of questioning. Either we tone it down or reconvene at a later date."

Roxanne softened a bit, but she continued to dissect the psychologist's report point by point. After a full twenty minutes of uneasiness and restlessness permeating the room, the psychologist requested that each attendee at the meeting return her photocopied evaluations. She said she would rewrite the assessment to reflect a need for a part-time aide.

I was flabbergasted and emotionally drained. The whole experience was difficult for me. After all, I was a teacher in this school district, and I had known most of these people on a professional level prior to this meeting. To make matters more uncomfortable, a teacher I worked with regularly was a close friend of the psychologist. I couldn't help but wonder, despite the district's confidentiality policy, if I'd feel a little tension back at the "office."

I also wondered how the psychologist felt as she sat stone-faced the whole time Roxanne laid into her. This lady, on the brink of her swan-song retirement, had just had her character thrown around the room like a dodge-ball in my PE class on a rainy day. It had to have hurt. But the bottom line was that the psychologist was flat out lying, and our advocate had called her on it. The principal knew it, as did everyone else in that room.

I don't totally fault the old veteran for her presentation of her so-called facts and figures. In my opinion, our school district is taught to offer the lowest possible amount of services in order to save a buck. I don't know how high up this unofficial mandate goes, but it's a tragedy that children who really need services have to go without them.

In the end, Riley was provided with a wonderful aide to start the third grade, and Lori and I were satisfied with the result of our IEP calamity.

It should be noted, though, that Roxanne was too good to be true:

She didn't return emails in a timely fashion—strike one.

Her bedside manner with Riley's support group (teacher and therapists) was cool at best—strike two.

And she was so gosh darn expensive! Strike three, you're OUT!

As I said, Roxanne produced good results, and I'd hire someone like her again if I were faced with something as important as Riley's (or Aidan's) IEP again, but thankfully, I don't anticipate needing services like hers in the near future.

I want to point out that I have a great respect for Riley's support team. Most of them are fantastic individuals, both in and out of school. They truly care about kids and want the best for them, but sometimes their hands are tied within the school system's mismanagement. Here, I blame the system, not the individuals.

26: T-ball: "Run, Boy, RUN!"

"I'LL TAKE RILEY to her softball, and you can take Aidan to his T-ball," I said nonchalantly but calculatingly. The truth of the matter is that I did not want to take Aidan to T-ball practice or games.

Aidan was six years old now, and for the past three years he had fought me to the last bitter whine when I'd offered any batting or throwing instruction. I'd hang in there, and his willingness to let me help him would increase, but it came with a price: my motivation.

An even colder truth, however, was that I had trouble watching Aidan play T-ball. It sounds terrible, but it hurt. It hurt knowing that Aidan could not seemingly understand what was asked of him. That he simply could not mindfully hit the ball and run to first base effectively. That he wasn't succeeding in ways the other kids could.

I know T-ball, and I know how to work with kids. I certainly think playing baseball throughout my youth

and being a PE teacher qualify me for aiding a kinder-
gartner. Yet Aidan gave me no slack. By this point, I was
well versed enough on Aidan's autism challenges that I
knew I had to get in and get out. For example, I'd show
him one or two quick tips on holding the bat and standing, then get the heck out of there before that five-second
window of opportunity closed and the Beast roared his
dissatisfaction.

After weeks of applying the techniques I'd learned
from OT (patience and common sense) to batting practice
at home, I got Aidan to the point where he could hit the
ball and feel good about doing it. But running to first base
was another matter.

So, the following Saturday morning, I gathered up the
T-ball equipment (tee, four bases, three balls, two gloves,
one bat, two water bottles, and a towel) and my enthusi-
asm. My daughters were somewhat willing to go along.
As I was about to find out, the formal act of an outing
interested them more than helping me teach Aidan to run
to first base. Lori supported my endeavor, but I think she
had her doubts.

We set up our baseball stuff at the local park's baseball diamond. I had Riley, then eight, demonstrate the
process of hitting the ball off the tee and running to first
base. Our extensive, yet sometimes reluctant, personal
trainer softball sessions together had apparently paid off
somewhat in this situation.

Aidan's eyes wandered, and I wasn't sure if he saw
Riley's feeble hit and skipping routine up the line. I asked

Riley to do it again, but she said she needed a drink of water first.

I said pleadingly, "C'mon, Riley. Just do it one more time to show Aidan what to do."

Riley did her lackluster stroll to the batter's box, and I made a mad dash to get the ball ready while begging for Aidan's focus and attention. Again, Aidan had barely caught half the instructional scene, and I knew Riley had had enough after just those two brief illustrations.

By now, Kira, my four-year-old, started to cry because the glove on her hand felt like a twenty-pound dumbbell. She threw her mitt down and followed Riley to the drinking fountain.

Okay, two down, but I've still got Lori, I said to myself as the water in my metaphorically half-full glass started to drain away.

I set up Aidan and made an apparent blunder by exceeding the five-second limit to his willingness for hands-on instruction. He let out his patented whine-groan, and I backed off.

"Hit the ball, Aidan!" I said eagerly.

Aidan smashed the ball and smiled. And then just stood there.

"Run to first base, like Riley did!" I yelled excitedly.

Aidan started running, and I galloped next to him like an old racehorse well past its prime. He reached first base, where Mommy greeted him with a high five as if he had just made the game-winning hit in the World Series.

Okay. Not bad. Now it was time for fielding. Yippeee! I quickly pulled Riley back into the fray and let an unrelenting Kira cry for her mommy in the dugout. Riley, to her credit, stayed on task long enough to show Aidan how to field a ground ball that I hit to her. However, she threw the ball over Lori's head at first base, which made her, then Aidan, giggle, thus losing our window of precious focus time.

Launching a verbal jab at Lori, I suggested that she could have jumped a little higher for the ball. She reciprocated by sending eye daggers in my direction. I sensed I was losing the team's continuity but trudged on nevertheless.

I hit a weak ground ball in Aidan's direction. It rolled to a stop, and he picked it up. He stared at it, said something incomprehensible, then threw a grounder to Lori. *Yes! Victory!* We did it three more times, and he repeated the same routine: pick up the ball, mumble, and throw it in Lori's direction. I praised Aidan for being able to follow the two-step process of fielding and throwing, but I was mystified by the deliberate pause and garbled speech he performed each time.

I looked at Lori and said, "What is he doing?"

Lori said, "I was trying to figure that out. I think he's reenacting the baseball game that he plays on the Wii."

Lori was right. Aidan was visualizing and pretending to be the character in the Wii baseball game that he'd been playing every afternoon for the last month.

With that knowledge I decided to gather the troops, highlight the positives, discard the negatives, and take them all out for doughnuts. Kira's stabbing cries turned to giddy laughter as Riley and Aidan ran to the car.

A few days later, Aidan, escorted by Lori, appeared ready for T-ball game number one. Meanwhile, I chaperoned an unwilling Kira to watch Riley's softball game, where Kira ceaselessly whined about not being able to go to the slide park across the way.

I felt extremely nervous for Lori (and for Aidan). Putting aside the dynamic of what other parents may observe or think, I sensed the demands would be too much for Aidan to handle. I feared Lori would have to suffer through one of Aidan's outbursts and end up going out onto the field to correct his behavior.

I couldn't wait to get home to hear the news about Aidan's game. I unabashedly asked Lori how it went.

"It went fine," she said casually as she shrugged her shoulders as if there wasn't any big deal.

"Huh?! What?! Details, m'lady. Details!" I said.

She responded, "Well, I did have to go onto the field because Aidan didn't like where he was supposed to stand, but he was pretty much in tune to each batter's hit. He knew to follow the team in and out of the dugout. And he followed the coach's instructions well. It does help that his coach is a special education teacher too, you know."

"Ahhhh, success!" I said, relieved, and I let out a deep breath.

After two more rather encouraging games, I felt it was finally my turn as Dad to take on one of Aidan's sporting events.

It started out okay. The coach gave the team a pep talk (Aidan didn't understand any of it, but he did stand idly by), and then the players ran out to their positions. The coach recognized me and said, "Hey, Kyle, how about coaching third base for us today?"

Oh, joy, I thought. *Just what I wanted to do while my real job being here is to monitor Aidan's stubborn-behavior-o-meter.*

"Sure, I'd be glad to!" I said, earning an Academy Award for best supporting actor.

Aidan was batting first in the lineup today, so I knew there wouldn't be any issues with him being upset that he wasn't allowed to hit in his timely manner (as Lori had suggested may happen).

Aidan dragged the bat on his meandering stroll to the batter's box and saddled up in his ready stance. He then drew back his bat, slowly but surely.

From my viewpoint at the third-base coaching position, I watched as he uncharacteristically gritted his teeth and took a mighty swing toward the teed ball.

SWOOOOSH! Swing and a miss.

No worries. I pondered as Aidan gripped his bat, eager for another try.

SWOOOOSH! Again he missed the ball.

No problem, I told myself. *Third time is the charm.* But I grew a little more anxious.

"It's okay, Aidan. Try again!" I yelled to him, not knowing if he heard me or not.

The coach went up to the plate, lowered the T-ball stand, and . . . *POWWW!* The swinging bat, unleashed in Aidan's oblivion, just missed striking the coach's hand! Aidan made solid contact, however, and the ball sailed through the pitcher's legs.

Aidan hurriedly ran to first base as I yelled, "Go, Aidan, Go!" I felt myself filling up with proud elation.

He stood at first base as if he'd been there a thousand times and listened to the first base coach's words. At least, it looked like he was listening.

The next batter was a girl named Makenna. She was the best hitter on the team. Makenna could really attack the ball, and I knew I'd be waving her around third base soon.

On her first swing, she crushed the ball over the left fielder's head. I could hear the first base coach tell Aidan to run to second base. Aidan clippity-clopped his way to second base, where he obediently stopped and ritualistically held his ground. The trouble was, Makenna was turning her drive into a double, and maybe more.

"Run, Aidan, RUN!" I shouted to him.

"No flippin' way," his body language told me. I knew what he was thinking. "I've run to second base each and every game, and every time I stop right here and wait for the next player to bat. I'm *stayin'*!"

Makenna passed Aidan up and kept on running. I circled my arm for her to keep going, and she greeted her cheering team at home plate.

In the meantime, other parents encouraged Aidan to run, but he still would have none of it. As he became even more irritated, I told the coach to just have the next batter hit.

After two more batters, I eventually gave my boy a thumbs-up at third base and told him to run home. (Actually, I specifically told him to run to the tee at home plate. If I just said, "Run home," who knows what would have happened?)

Lori and I took the next year off from organized baseball for Aidan. We're glad that he had the opportunity to participate and complete the season, but we felt that we'd direct our efforts elsewhere for a while. Each game held a challenge for him as well as for us. Initially we were happy that Aidan was able to learn and to further his social and emotional development, but sometimes you've just gotta take a break for your own sanity.

27: Potty Time!

"WHAT'S THAT SMELL?" I said to Lori from the kitchen.

"I think it's Aidan," she said.

Aidan was happily playing the Wii in the living room. I walked over and questioned him. "Did you poop your pants?"

He replied with a grin, "Noooooo."

I stretched the back of his pants back from the waist to take a look, and . . .

Yep, he'd crapped his pants. At six years old, he'd had an accident while playing a video game. Or had he? Fortunately or unfortunately, depending on how you look at it, we eventually figured out that Aidan was consciously choosing not to go potty in the bathroom. We caught him in the act. The scenario looked like this:

He'd be in a full potty dance and we'd ask him, "Do you need to go to the bathroom?"

He'd respond, "No."

We'd qualify by saying, "Are you sure?"

"Yessss," came the reply.

Then I'd check his pants. Nothing there. Five minutes later, Aidan would continue with his bathroom boogie and I'd repeat the questioning. And lo and behold, chocolate bar central.

It appeared he was just too into his game to make the effort of going to the bathroom. Frankly, I felt he was being plain lazy. And I was mad at our little guy.

Let me back up to a bit, to when Aidan was four, and set the stage. Our research told us that it was common for autistic children to be late bloomers in the "going potty" department. It was also common for them to be bed wetters. Figuring he'd get it eventually, I wasn't too concerned at the time. However, the more we worked with Aidan, the more I worried that going potty could be a life-long problem.

So, Aidan's ABA service set a goal for him: to go potty on his own, during daytime hours, at a minimum 80 percent success rate, within one week. To accomplish this feat, they did what was called a potty party. They basically held Aidan's daily four-hour session in the bathroom for five consecutive days. Every time Aidan did his thing in the toilet, the ABA tutor and supervisor jumped up and had Aidan join them in a celebratory potty cheer and dance. Then Aidan would get to devour his favorite food: a Hostess CupCake.

Aidan was hooked on the potty party, and the strategy worked. And once he learned to go potty by himself routinely, the extrinsic rewards were reduced until he no longer relied on them. It only took *six months* (heavy sarcasm here) to get from no potty skills whatsoever to almost perfect daytime potty mastery. In all seriousness, we were thrilled to accomplish this mission. Thank you, ABA.

But it wasn't that easy to get to the half-year mark in Aidan's milestone achievement. After ABA completed its crash course in toilets for tots, Lori and I implemented the use of something I hope to never use again: a kitchen timer. On the advice of ABA, we had the timer go off every thirty minutes. We'd dutifully separate Aidan from whatever he was doing (yes, tantrums were involved), dispense his three gulps of liquid, and escort our reluctant little boy to the toilet. It would take him a minute to adjust to his fate, and then he would sit for ten minutes and hum a Raffi (children's music) tune. Riley and Kira were more than content to remind Aidan, in their sisterly way, that it was his potty time whenever that incessant timer went off. This process went on every single day for a month. Then ABA cleared us to move to every hour on the hour for the next month, every two hours for the third month, and on and on until potty-trained bliss graced us all. In those grueling months, that poor kid must have drunk more water than a first-year college student consumes in beer.

Nighttime, on the other hand, was a completely different matter. At age seven, Aidan was still wearing Pull-Ups for bed-wetting. Amid all the other issues we were dealing with, Lori and I finally motivated ourselves to take a stand. We adamantly agreed, "The Pull-Ups are gone. If Aidan wets his bed wearing only underwear, so be it. *He'll learn.*"

Well, we are the ones learning. Learning to wash his sheets every morning for a month. Learning to clean up Aidan and get him in fresh underwear at 3 a.m., when he wakes up feeling uncomfortable.

We feel like we've covered the basics over the past few years. Aidan has been restricted from drinking any liquids before bedtime, has been rewarded with praises and stickers for being dry the next morning, and has taken ownership by creating an a.m. "I'm Dry!" chart to log his accomplishments. We've even played it hardcore on him by not allowing him to play his Wii on days when he isn't completely dry. Nighttime bed-wetting has improved, but it's a work in progress for now.

Now, back to Aidan's unwillingness to comply with his daytime number-two potty duties during a highly preferred activity time, such as the Wii or his Legos.

The solution? The Wii was immediately turned off. Aidan was briskly marched to the bathroom to clean up the mess *himself* (under my direction), verbally reprimanded in my strictest tone (again), and then sent off to his room for a ten-minute time-out with the door firmly closed. We performed this act together about five times (one day it happened twice!), and he eventually got the message. We haven't had a mishap (cross your fingers) since. Sometimes some simple, good old-fashioned parenting is just what Aidan needs. As far as the daytime issue is concerned, we feel we're officially on the road to potty recovery.

28: Managing Autism with Siblings

SINCE WE'RE ON the subject of challenges, let's explore how an autistic brother finds his way among his two charismatic sisters. I'm sure sibling rivalries exist in every household, and ours is no different. However, there just might be an additional conflict or two to deal with in our neck of the woods. And the confrontations seem to last a little longer, without the satisfaction of a happy, rational ending.

As I mentioned, our daughter Riley has ADD and a mild form of PDD-NOS, and while these conditions are certainly not great gifts for her, they haven't exactly been advantageous to the rest of us either. She is now nine years old, and we feel she should be demonstrating a reasonable ability to solve problems in a social setting. We're also thinking she should rise above amateur status because she has been in social-group classes for two years now. These one-hour, weekly classes are set up for a group of three children who lack fundamental social skills. The gatherings are conducted by a licensed family therapist in a clinical setting, in which she facilitates proper social etiquette when children are engaged in group situations. Still, we are constantly practicing conflict resolution with Riley and Aidan. Lately I've even been thinking that I should record my next postgame talk with her, so all I have to do is press PLAY for future meetings, thus saving my breath.

Let me provide you with this example:

Riley is watching her favorite TV program. I say, "Hey, Riley. We're trying to teach Aidan to use his words when he wants to play the Wii game. When your show ends, can you respond appropriately when we have him ask you if he can play the Wii?"

Riley apathetically responds, "Okay."

I anxiously use my small window of opportunity to gain Aidan's eye contact and Riley's glazed stare. "All right, Aidan. Ask Riley if you can play the Wii."

Aidan obediently complies. "Riley, can I play the Wii."

Riley plainly replies, "No, Aidan. I'm watching. Go away."

What the #@&#?!

Flabbergasted, I say, "Riley! You could have said any number of appropriate responses—'In five minutes, Aidan' or 'I'm almost done, Aidan' or 'Sure, Aidan. Thanks for asking nicely.'"

Riley and I have had the Autism Talk several times. I sat her down in her room, away from any distractions, and we discussed what autism is. I explained how her brother has trouble expressing himself and how we need to help him find the words. We also role-played helping Aidan politely request what he wants. We further talked about how we may have to tolerate some odd behavior if we find that Aidan is in a "learning moment."

I do realize that this is some heavy stuff to rest on a third grader, but we're trying to instill in Riley some compassion and acceptance for Aidan, as well as to put her in a leadership position in the hope that she will rise to the occasion.

There are times when Riley is an absolute rock star. A big-time creator of abstract design, she will periodically approach Aidan and say, "Hey, Aidan, do you want to see my new invention?"

Aidan has no idea what *invention* means, but we are thrilled that Riley is engaging her brother. And after she invites him to join her, for the next hour, Riley and Aidan are BFFs as they explore her man-made waterfall comprised of Daddy's backyard hose, scrap wood from the side of the house, boxes from the garage, and yard chairs that I just folded up for the winter.

The really rocky relationship is the one between Aidan and his younger sister, Kira. The love-hate episodes these two have are momentous. One day they are jumping onto huge beanbags from a table in our family room (converted sensory room) and giggling nonstop for forty-five minutes; the next moment they are simultaneously crying and yelling at each other as if someone knocked over their double-scoop chocolate ice cream cones.

Kira is one sharp cookie, though. Her language skills rival Riley's (four years older) and surpass Aidan's. While she tends to have an unreasonable temperament when she misses her daily nap, Kira can heroically be our eyes and ears by relaying needed information about what Aidan does or does not do when he can't explain it himself.

A few years ago, a friend of mine shed some positive light on my children's sibling situation. Only weeks after Aidan's diagnosis, I did my best to thwart my melancholy. But a fellow teacher, Larry, who was unaware of my dilemma, apparently saw right through me. He said, "What's up, Kyle? I noticed you haven't been your chipper self these days. What's going on?"

I thought I was a good actor at the time, but I decided to confide in Larry, who had always been a straight shooter and a strong voice of reason in our faculty meetings. I told him that I had recently learned that my son had autism and I was coming to grips with the matter. I said things like, "I just don't know what it's going to look like for him when he gets older" and "The future may not be forgiving for kids with these issues."

Then he said something that was like a prophecy for me. "Aidan has a younger sister, right?"

"Yes," I said. "She's a little go-getter."

He seemed to spin his thinking wheels for a moment, and then he said, "You won't have to worry. She will be the one who will someday look after your son."

Almost three years have passed since that brief conversation with Larry. And wouldn't you know, things are shaping up along those lines: Kira is becoming a caregiver to Aidan.

Just last week I made a bold move and entered Aidan and Kira in a basketball clinic for ages four to six. Kira was four and a half going on seven, and Aidan was seven going on who knows.

The setup was perfect. The class numbers were low, and Aidan didn't feel compelled to hide in his figurative fetal position. I then witnessed what I hope is a foreshadowing of Aidan and Kira's relationship for years to come.

The coach instructed the kids to dribble their basketballs to the wall and back. I caught Aidan staring out toward Never Never Land—he obviously hadn't gotten the memo on what to do. Kira made the read on Aidan's malfunction, gently grabbed Aidan's hand, and motioned for him to dribble with her. Aidan smiled and might as well have skipped on air as he triumphantly followed his sister. I was a proud parent at that moment.

The supportiveness continued as Mama Bird Kira pointed and guided Aidan appropriately throughout the hour. And we made it a point to tell Mommy what a great helper Kira was with Aidan. Kira was absolutely beaming as she proudly relayed the news. And I had ESP-like visions of a future Kira, in her twenties, calling Aidan to remind him about his DMV appointment and Grandma's upcoming birthday.

As a trio, Riley is the idea maker, Kira is the organizer, and Aidan is the happy follower. There are times when the three of them are absent of any ADD, authoritativeness, and autism. They can work like army ants creating a trail of pillows down the hall or swim like friendly dolphins in our backyard pool. Then, from out of nowhere, Aidan's quirkiness, Riley's social idiosyncrasies, and Kira's Napoleonic leadership skills collide in a perfect storm. Lori and I have seconds to man the sails, and BOOM! Too late. Aidan's flipping out because Riley won't "share" (that is, surrender) the balloon that she just blew up for Kira. Kira is yelling at Aidan because of his high-pitched scream. Aidan, now upset with Kira, swipes his hand on her shoulder in what is not quite a slap. The touch barely grazes her body, yet Kira starts bawling because she's four. All the while Riley doesn't seem to care. She easily could have judged the situation and simply given Aidan another balloon to end his frustration, since she has an entire bag of them, but instead she strolls off to create more abstract art with her balloons.

Does this kind of affair happen routinely? You betcha! It goes in spurts, but it's fair to say that our kids are a bit more susceptible to these types of occurrences than most.

Now some of you may be thinking, "You've got to lay down the law with your children. Establish those boundaries!"

My response is simple: "You just don't get it." Structure in any family environment is important, and I'm sure we could use more, but if you were a fly on the wall in our home, you'd know why we have to choose our battles carefully: we're tired!

But we'll always get up for the next day. Carpe diem!

29: Autism Families Become Our Circle of Friends

I GREW UP with a variety of friends. As an identical twin, I had double the pals, since everybody my brother met instantly became someone I knew, and vice versa. I also played sports throughout my youth, and this opened up another realm of buddies to hang out with. Couple that with a college experience at Chico State University (yes, the rumors are true) and a fraternity to boot, and you've got the makings for plenty of lasting friendships.

But my friendship base faded exponentially with the birth of each child. My responsibilities inevitably changed (meaning I actually *had* responsibilities), and the spontaneous social gatherings become less regular and more structured. Kids' birthday parties, Fourth of July barbecues, and block parties became my primary social events.

The new friendships Lori and I now develop are generally results of our kids' activities or special educational needs.

We held Aidan's seventh birthday at the bowling alley. He had seven friends there: Josh, who used to be in his special day class; Ryan, who used to be in his communicative handicap class; Aditiya, was a family friend's autistic child; and four teacher-picked students from his first-grade general-ed classroom.

The parents of the four neurotypical children were very nice, but it was clear that we did not have much in common when it came to our kids. Their children were self-sufficient when it came to peer play. They could wander off to the far reaches of a playground with a buddy or draw with chalk in the backyard without supervision. On the other hand, the Aidans, Joshes, Ryans and Aditiyas of the world needed constant surveillance. This understandably created a divide in what our children could share together, let alone in the lasting personal connections they could establish with one another at this time. The situation also made it difficult for us parents to form any consistent ties.

When Lori joined a mommies' group for children on the autistic spectrum soon after Aidan's diagnosis, it opened up a wide variety of newfound relationships. She and Aidan would meet other families at a park, at the zoo, at bouncy houses, and at birthday parties. Lori especially appreciated not having to explain when a child was scripting (discussed in chapter 19), hand flapping in the corner, or having an hour-long meltdown. Everyone there knew exactly what everyone else was going through. So I guess you could say that we were all being haphazardly pulled along in the same tugboat. Lori also valued being able to bounce ideas off the other moms while sharing a few personal and heartfelt stories about what she was going through. It sounded like something I wouldn't want to attend—too much gushing and *feelings* for this average guy. Yet, after four and a half years, Lori continues to feel unequivocally at home with the group.

I can definitely understand why Lori feels comfortable going to her group. Most of them are probably having the same thoughts about their respective children:

- Is my child exploring—i.e., roaming too far?
- Is he eating something he shouldn't be eating? Sand, perhaps?
- Is he acting appropriately? For instance, is he shoving someone down the slide because he didn't notice that the kid was patiently waiting for the person ahead of him to finish?
- Is my child being bullied? Has he become a victim because he cannot effectively express himself?

It is comforting to share a link with these other families. It helps to know that while we struggle, others have made it through the same situations—and to know that no matter what pain we are suffering, a similar family can show us how to confront it successfully.

And while our fellow parents of special-needs kids are well versed about OT, PT, speech therapy, ABA, and IEPs, we'd all like to expand our terminology outside that special-needs box through more playdates, parks-and-rec activities, and music lessons. We'd also like to make more contacts beyond our special education realm.

Toward the end of Aidan's first regular-ed classroom experience (with his full-time aide), we noticed that he had developed an association that seemed a bit more meaningful than merely playing with someone on the playground at lunchtime.

A kindhearted classmate named Nick invited Aidan to his birthday party, and their association grew into something more than a teacher-facilitated four-square game at recess. We soon worked out a plan to have this new buddy of Aidan's join him at his playgroup twice a week, and they developed a special kinship.

Through Aidan's unique bond with Nick, Lori and I added two companions to our circle of friends: Nick's parents.

And I don't think they even know what an IEP is, which is certainly okay with us.

30: My Day as an Autistic Seven-Year-Old, by Aidan Wilkin

NOTE: THIS CHAPTER is my lighthearted attempt to perceive my son's life through his eyes.

2 a.m. *My day begins.*

I wet my bed. It doesn't bother me *that* much, but now I'm awake. So I walk into Mommy and Daddy's room and climb into their bed. Dad says to go to the bathroom, so I do. Mom then cleans me up and helps me put on dry underwear. I make another attempt to ascend their bed, and this time Dad pulls the covers down for me so I can snuggle in. I hear them snoring before I even settle in for my remaining slumber. They must be really tired.

7:00 a.m. *Good morning.*

I wake up with a smile on my face as I jab my knee into Daddy's back. I roll out of bed, run down the hallway to claim the TV before my sisters get to it, and play my favorite game: the Wii.

7:30 a.m.   *Wii time continues.*

After a half hour of playing *Super Mario Bros.*, my sister asks if she can play too. I curtly brush her off. My dad tries every strategy to get me to use my words, but I just don't care, 'cause it's *my* Wii and no one else can have it.

7:31 a.m.   *Breakfast.*

Without blinking an eye, Dad turns off the Wii and tells my sisters and me to sit at the table for breakfast. We all get something different. I like an apple-cinnamon frozen waffle, cut up to my specifications, with an ample amount of syrup. And don't even try slipping a blueberry waffle past me. They might look similar, but I'll push the blueberry one away like yesterday's oatmeal and won't eat a bite. No way, no how!

7:35 a.m.   *Track meet.*

I realize it's Dad's turn to take a shower as Mom and Dad sprint past each other. Mom has our clothes in her hands as she preoccupies our attention by turning the TV back on. I like TV, as long as I get to pick the channel.

7:50 a.m.   *Dad gets involved.*

Dad is back, and he tries to help get us all dressed. He doesn't have Mom's multitasking skills, so he turns off the TV and drives me and my sisters crazy mad.

8:00 a.m. *Mom finishes getting us dressed.*

8:05 a.m. *Independent preparation.*

I reluctantly go to the bathroom to wash my hands and brush my teeth. I've practiced this process countless times with ABA, so I decide to recite the steps out loud.

8:10 a.m. *Group preparation.*

Mom sprays water in my hair with a spray bottle and begins brushing it. I really hate that spray bottle. I become easily agitated and tersely blurt out my parents' favorite word: "Nooooo!"

Mom hands me the brush, and I rake my hair forward 'cause I think it looks cool. Dad drops in, takes the brush from me, and brushes my hair straight back. This disturbs me big-time 'cause I wasn't anticipating the brush strokes against my scalp—and 'cause he messes up the awesome do I had going. Then Dad abruptly leaves, and Mom fixes it as usual.

8:15 a.m. *The car.*

Mom puts my lunch in my backpack, and I make my way to the car. My older sister and I push and shove each other and say mean things as we make a mad dash to see who can open the car door first.

8:20 a.m.   *Arrive at school.*

I leap out of the car and race to my class line to drop off my backpack. I'm fired up that I have a minute to go down the slide at the playground. I always run, not 'cause I'm always late, but because I love school—once I'm there.

8:25 a.m.   *In class.*

I sit at my desk, and my aide says hi to me. She follows me wherever I go. She's like my special helper. I need her a lot 'cause I don't understand half the stuff the teacher says to do. We start with some number stuff they call math. I'm good at memorizing stuff, so I like math.

10:10 a.m.   *Recess.*

Recess is pretty cool. I usually play by myself on the monkey bars or shoot baskets. Once in a while an adult will bring another student over to play with me, which makes me feel good.

10:20 a.m.   *Back in Room 7.*

I yell at my aide 'cause she keeps telling me to write down my favorite color, and I barely know what *favorite* means. Besides that, I'm preoccupied with the fact that I cannot find my crayons in my desk and no one seems to care. And to top it off, I get even more frustrated 'cause she doesn't seem to understand me, so I throw myself on the floor and whine while the whole class looks at me. Why did they have to stop art so unexpectedly anyway?

11:50 a.m. *Lunch.*

Jeez-o-pete! It's noisy in this big room! I put my hands over my ears practically every day in this place. Some days I think I'm getting used to it, but today it's sooooo louuuuud! I try to eat my lunch, which always has stuff I like in it. It's like magic.

12:10 a.m. *Playtime after lunch.*

My sister Riley comes over to play with me. I think she's a little shy and doesn't have many friends to play with, so she likes to join me. I like seeing her. We go acorn collecting by the big oak tree.

1:50 p.m. *End-of-school bell.*

I'm finally getting used to the bells at school. I'm glad to see my mom pick me up, but I'd really like to stay at school for now. My aide hands my mom a piece of paper about my day and says that I earned a green apple, which is really just a green piece of paper in the shape of an apple. I guess I had good day 'cause both my aide and Mommy are smiling at me.

2:30 p.m. *ABA.*

My ABA tutor works with me for three hours on life-skill stuff. I'm getting tired at this point, but I've been doing this for almost three years now, so I know I'll make it through.

5:30 p.m. *My dad.*

Dad comes home, and I jubilantly say, "Daddy, you're baaack!" He takes me outside to shoot some baskets. I know he's trying to help me shoot the ball correctly, but I want him to just let me shoot it. So I jerk the ball away from him and give him a modest scream. Then he simply stands there until I calm down. And behold, he tries again.

6:00 p.m. *Dinner.*

My parents are always trying to put something different on my plate. Don't they know that I just want a hot dog or nuggets and nothing else? Yeah, water is fine, but don't even think about putting it in a pink cup. That's for girls!

6:45 p.m. *Homework time.*

I read some spelling words with Mom. I can remember words okay, but I don't know what most of them mean. Dad is doing homework with Riley. I think he thinks it's easier to work with her, but I still like it when he reads to me before bedtime.

7:00 p.m. *Listening therapy time.*

I ask Mom if I can play on the computer, but she says I have to wear my headphones too. Then she says, "First jammies, then computer." I comply 'cause I know how she works. She lays out my clothes and a Pull-Up. I'm back to wearing Pull-Ups 'cause I still wet my bed.

Someday I'll figure it out, but for now, I just don't care enough to worry about it.

7:30 p.m. *Dessert.*

I call out in a speedy voice, "I WANT CHOCOLATE ICE CREAM!" and hope that my parents hear me. Dad comes back with my tasty treat in his hand and takes a lick before handing it over. That dirty rat! He always says he has to taste it first to make sure it's safe, but I don't know what he's talking about. Then he won't let go of it until I look right at him and say, "Thank you."

8:00 p.m. *Sister playtime.*

I make pillow forts with my sisters. We laugh as we tumble to the ground. My little sister, Kira, usually ends up crying, and I've learned to say to her, "Are you okaaay?" Sometimes I don't mean it, but I've been taught what to say in these situations, so I say it.

8:30 p.m. *First attempt at bedtime.*

Mom and Dad try to get us to go to the bathroom to brush teeth, wash hands, and eventually go to bed. It doesn't work out for them.

8:45 p.m. *Sleep potion.*

Mom gives us liquid melatonin.

9:00 p.m. *Second attempt at bedtime.*

Mom and Dad are still trying to get us to go to the bathroom to brush teeth, wash hands, and get off to bed. Sorry, guys—not gonna happen.

9:01 p.m. *Third and final attempt.*

I'm tired. I go to the bathroom to brush my teeth and wash my hands, step by step. Then I swagger down the hallway to my bedroom. Dad lies with me for five minutes while telling me about tomorrow's agenda as I drift off to sleep.

Good night, everyone. See you at 2 a.m.

31: Why Me?

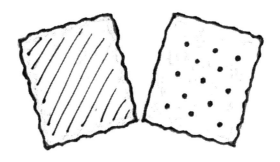

IT'S IN MY face every day.

I see it while getting the kids ready for school, dropping them off at their classrooms, looking in the eyes of the students I teach, coaching basketball, attempting to get a babysitter (which actually happens once in a blue moon), meeting other parents' children, and walking through the door after an overwhelming day at the factory (aka junior high school):

My boy has autism.

Even now, after years of nonstop therapy for Aidan and structuring our lives around the best possible situations for our kids, I can't let go of the question, "How could this have happened to me?"

Some may call it selfishness to dwell on how this all affects me, but they don't walk in my shoes, so frankly, they can stick it! I'm fairly sure my reaction is natural. And while I've continued to move forward as best I can and have never indulged in playing the blame game, I believe I can sensibly and rightfully say (like most dads experiencing this journey), "Autism sucks!"

Do I persistently feel this way? No way! My days are probably just as satisfying as they are for the regular Joe. I get fired up for fantasy football and my San Francisco Giants and 49ers like any other guy, but I still have my worries about what life has in store for my boy—and me. I guess every parent does. I just feel like my worries are a little different and maybe even more potent than some other people's worries. And yet, I know there are others out there with much bigger hardships than mine.

Even if I did play the blame game, where would I turn?

I don't blame the government or the System. I don't blame my wife or our parents. I don't secretly blame myself. And yes, I did look upward and question the Big Guy. But all in all, I don't point a finger at anyone. For a lack of a better phrase, it is what it is.

You can bet I occasionally look over the proverbial fence at the green grass, where my twin brother's boys are attending Boy Scout meetings, going to music lessons, and hitting home runs on their Little League teams. That seems like a pretty good life, while I'm busy teaching my son not to throw a fit just because the cracker I gave him has a design that's different from the one on the crackers he's used to. ("It's the *same* cracker, Aidan!")

But from a dad's perspective, I have dreams about moments and activities I want to share with my son, and it's very tough to know that I simply won't be able to enjoy what I now see so many other parents take for granted.

And know this about me: I'm a realist. I knew that all five feet eight inches of me wasn't going to pass along a genetically gifted, athletic superstar body, but having so many doors closed on my boy due to this mysterious disorder has had an overwhelming effect on me. How could it not?

It's true what they say: time does heal. I get better at dealing with our special set of challenges every day. And furthermore, this father will never, ever give up supporting or loving his son. Yes, expectations have been altered, and new benchmarks have been set. I've been forced to accept this life-changing experience, regardless of whether or not I've wanted to adjust or even felt capable of it. And to keep my sanity, I've learned quickly in this expedition to appreciate the joys Aidan experiences and to support him in all of his interests. Isn't that what all good dads would do for their kids?

And along the way I came to the realization that I didn't have to go it alone. Early on in this journey, my friend Steve approached me with some advice that may have changed me forever. A spiritual man, he suggested that I confer with the Almighty for solace while grappling with all of my unanswerable questions.

I was by no means a nonbeliever, but it had been a long time since I had really asked the Lord for anything. A few days passed after my brief exchange with Steve, and while I didn't officially address my plight with God, the thought wouldn't escape my mind. I wasn't trying to shake it off or anything, but whenever I had a break in my workday, there seemed to be a knock on my internal door.

So that night I rested my weary head on my pillow, and I asked God some questions—lots of 'em. I asked him why this all had happened, why I was the so-called lottery winner, and why I had been chosen to take this path. *Why me, God?*

I fell asleep amid my enquiries. When I woke up the next morning I felt surprisingly restful, a sensation I hadn't had in a long time. My questions hadn't really been resolved, but in an odd sort of way I felt a little better about my state of affairs.

The next night I asked God for Aidan to get better. I believe I solicited that for the next ten days and found myself even more relaxed prior to drifting off to sleep each of those nights. It was a peculiar phenomenon: as my relationship with God grew, my demeanor became calmer. I was more at ease about aspects of my situation that used to frustrate me.

Yet on my next night of talking to God, something struck my heart (or was it my soul?). *When have I ever thanked him?* I thought. *When have I ever thanked God for what I have in my life? When have I showed him my appreciation for all the good things that have happened to me?* That evening I lay back and I *prayed*. I thanked God for my wife and children. I thanked him for the love we shared as a family. I thanked him for my parents and for all the learning experiences that helped form the person I had become. I made it a point not to ask him for anything that night. I wanted to express only the gratitude I had for him.

The next evening I felt a little more comfortable asking. I didn't just ask for Aidan this time. I asked for all my children. I asked for Lori. I asked for my family. Then, after a few weeks, I ultimately asked for me. I asked God for strength to handle my situation. I asked him for patience and tolerance. I asked him to bless me with the qualities of a good husband and father.

Then I thanked him.

I guess I will always hold on to the hope that some great discovery will enable Aidan to have all of the opportunities that so many other kids have today. I know there's got to be a balance between wishful thinking and practicality, but I hope always to remain open to the power of prayer.

In the end, my son's autism is really not about just me; it's about supporting my son and offering all the love I have for the children in my blessed family.

32: Phillip and Company: The Autism Learning Curve

THE SCENE: WATER cooler chat time in the boys' locker room office

The characters: PE teachers and assistant principal

The pinnacle: Wilkin gets upset. *Very* upset.

The gathering started out ordinarily enough. A few of us PE teachers were casually venting about the antics of our middle school students. Our assistant principal, Rick, paid us a visit and was soon supplying us with even more fuel for our self-made fires. I contributed to the rant by telling a story about a boy named Phillip.

Phillip was new to our school, and although he wasn't in my class, I had noticed his mischievous nature. He was a bit of a loner and had a crafty way about him. Phillip seemed to be the type of kid who was always fiddling inside his backpack and being out of the area he was supposed to be in.

Here is the Phillip story I told my colleagues:

Last week, some of Phillip's fellow students alerted me that he had wandered off from the locker room and was in the gym by himself (which was against school rules). I marched my high-ranking authority through the gym doors and found him standing there, looking up at the lights.

With my best disapproving look and most imposing tone, I said, "What are you doing in here, bud?"

Phillip peered at me without much of a care and shrugged his shoulders.

You can bet I was unimpressed with his apathetic reaction to my question, so I curtly told him, "I don't want to see you roaming around in here again. Get in the locker room with everybody else."

I later asked Phillip's PE teacher, Jessica, about him.

Here is a quick side note for all parents who want some inside information. If you want to know how your kids *really* are at school—I'm referring to their true character, including integrity, honesty, respect for authority and peers, and whether they are putting forth sincere effort—just ask their PE and elective teachers.

Jessica shook her head discouragingly and plainly said, "Something's not quite right with him. He sometimes seems to blow off my instructions and chooses to do them only in his own good time."

Now, I was feeling not too thrilled with this boy. I'm known as a compassionate and fair teacher, but my patience for students who actively defy school rules is limited. In my mind, this kid has a bad attitude.

As I was telling this story to my fellow PE teachers and the assistant principal, each member of our group reacted with a grimacing nod, as if to say, "I've heard this type of tale a hundred times before."

Rick listened attentively, while simultaneously monitoring calls on his earpiece, and then raised an eyebrow in a perplexed look. I assumed he was equally dismayed by this child's lack of respect as I talked about Phillip's attitude.

Finding such a supportive reaction to my story, I continued. By now I was standing up, because I just can't seem to tell stories without getting animated and dramatic to engage my audience.

The next day another group of students told me that Phillip was meandering outside when he was supposed to be getting dressed in the locker room.

I jumped from my chair and took my disdain for Phillip's behavior with me. I found him pitching rocks at the side of an equipment shed and making a loud ka-boom with each toss.

"Hey!" I bellowed, thirty feet from Phillip. He nonchalantly turned in my direction with an odd smirk on his face. Now I was mad. This kid flatly didn't give a crap.

I got up near his face and took in his unemotional gaze. It was as if he were telling me he wasn't interested in what I had to say to him. I started blasting him about his lack of character and asking what gave him the right to damage school property.

He just stood there taking it all in, while offering no reasons for his actions. I flippantly told him to go inside. As he strolled off, I took a deep breath, shook my head, and wondered what was up with the youth today.

With my story over, my PE cohorts offered more supportive remarks: "What a piece of work." "Who's his teacher again?" "Did you call his parents yet?"

Then Rick chimed in with a matter-of-fact tone. "You know, he's a nonverbal autistic," he said.

"What?!" I exploded.

I couldn't believe what I had just heard. I was beside myself with anger, in addition to feeling like a complete doofus.

"Rick!" I blurted. "I just worked this kid over, and I had no idea he was autistic!"

Rick read my feelings of despair and said, "Don't beat yourself up over this. You didn't know."

"And that's why I'm frickin' pissed off! How in the hell can you or the counselor, or someone in our dang office, not alert the teachers about Phillip?" I exclaimed.

Our discussion—a one-sided argument, really—ended with someone calling it a drop of the ball by the school office and saying that it wouldn't likely happen again.

I only became even more distraught with how a school (and maybe even Phillip's parents) could be so irresponsible and careless as to not provide such critical information to those who could support Phillip—let alone simply come into contact with him.

This issue punched me in the gut for the rest of the school year. I'm not normally one to lose it like that with a student, and, rest assured, I figured I owed it to Phillip to look after his interest for the remainder of his stay at our school.

While I was a rookie to autism at the time, I was still disappointed in myself for not recognizing the signs Phillip displayed—communicative handicap, social awkwardness, inappropriate body language, and unresponsiveness—regardless of the autism label.

Of course, not all autistic kids have these symptoms, but they are certainly common on the autistic spectrum—thus the need for services to support these children!

This incident occurred about the time Aidan was born. Since then, I have learned that autism can be a hidden disorder. It is not always easily identified and can be perceived as someone simply being odd, weird, or even rude. I believe they place autism on a spectrum because there are so many different "shades" of how the disorder is manifested. While Aidan is verbal and Phillip is not, they are both considered to be high functioning due to some of their "normal" abilities.

Eight years have passed since that big aha moment for me. Our school now has two fully aided autism classes. And recently, our staff had an in-service meeting conducted by our district BSP (behavioral specialist), notifying us that autism is on the rise and that "these children will be fully included in our classrooms in the future." In other words, they were telling us to get used to it and to be prepared. Thankfully, teachers at my school are recognizing that their students with autism have varying degrees of the disorder.

Another example of the innumerable variations on this spectrum was a really cool kid in one of my classes. Michael was a die-hard fan of rock music and dancing. He was totally social, yet totally autistic. His main quirk was the habit of unknowingly invading others' personal space, so he had to be reminded to "back up." While Michael had plenty of misunderstandings and social misfires, he still blended in with the climate of the school just fine. As I watched him grow into a capable kid over three years of middle school, I couldn't help but hope my Aidan would find his way as Michael had.

John also illustrates the broad diversity of autism. An avid runner (the best on our cross-country team), John had friends galore. While he had his share of misreads, he was good-natured and always smiling, and thus he had a buddy wherever he went. It was clear that his classmates knew he was a bit different, but due to his congenial way, everyone accepted him.

Michael and John were very high functioning, but that's not always the case. Take Tanner, for example. (Yep, they're all boys—go figure!) Tanner was neither jovial nor social. He was extremely introverted and had some anger-management issues. Yet he made it through our junior high school unscathed, for the most part. I tried connecting with him when he was mainstreamed into my PE class, but I found that he preferred to maintain a large zone of personal space. I respected that, but I still included him as much as he could tolerate. His aides were very supportive, and they taught me to appreciate what we could do with Tanner when we kept appropriate expectations and goals in mind.

As I said in chapter 23, it has always amazed me that some parents of autistic children try to hide the disorder from their children's peers and teachers. I get the fact that they want their child to be treated like everyone else; however, they don't realize that this way of thinking can be highly detrimental to their children's well-being in the school environment. Learning the hard way does not always translate into learning the most prosperous way. As in Phillip's scenario, teachers can provide a wealth of support for special-needs children and can facilite their interactions with peers—*as long as the teachers are clued in to the children's needs.*

In one of my classes, for example, I had a confident, overzealous thirteen-year-old boy named Will. Basically, he bebopped around like he owned the gym, and I would have to keep him in check regarding who actually ran the show. The interesting thing about this neurotypical but impulsive little guy was that he was kind to everybody, which is not a common trait among middle school kids. Therefore, I took advantage of this encouraging circumstance.

One day we were making teams in our PE class. Usually I would give the kids thirty seconds to divide themselves into small groups and then sit down in rows. As time wound down, I would inevitably make a mad dash to place shy students on teams to avoid any hurt feelings. But this time I tried something different.

I approached Will in advance and requested that he ask Jeremy, a reserved special-needs boy who flew under the radar with his peers, to be on his team.

When I blew the whistle for the team making to commence, Jeremy stood in his usual position and awaited my brisk stroll to his location. But instead, Will's energetic voice rang cheerfully in my ears: "Hey, Jeremy! Join us over here!"

The look on Jeremy's face was priceless. I could see him fill up with importance as he sat in Will's line. He played it off well, but I could see he felt powerfully significant.

From my first year of teaching, I made a concerted effort to support students who didn't quite have the self-assured personalities that others had. Now, with the increased number of special-needs students arriving in my classroom each year, coupled with my newfound hyperawareness of the trials of autism, I am proud to offer an accepting, tolerant, and compassionate environment for all special-needs children. And after the toll I took in Phillip's situation, the least I can do in my remaining years is to make a positive difference in kids' lives.

33: Hey, Honey, They Found Another Cure for Autism!

THERE IS SO much garbage on the Internet. And it probably got a boost from the new flavor of the month/year/decade: autism.

When Lori and I entered our first year of the autism experience, we were Internet sponges. I was so open to all the creative "cures" for autism that I gave our new credit card a whirl of a good time.

I purchased a special liquid supplement that was guaranteed to be as safe as Grandma's cough medicine, but that didn't work. Later I bought a quart of some nasty-tasting, orangey-yellow grog with a fluorescent sheen, but that was useless. And finally Aidan and I both tried a natural powder that came highly recommended from another parent of an autistic child.

The testimonials and stories were so compelling. This one guy claimed to have given his younger brother a "sacral massage" and miraculously cured him of his autistic ailments. He said that his brother started speaking considerably better and became more socially aware.

After my gullibility on that one, I cannot believe I seriously told Lori that we should look into getting Aidan a massage for his cranium. Lori rolled her eyes at that one, but I couldn't resist rubbing Aidan's scalp at bedtime—*just once*. (By the way, it just made him annoyed with me.)

Some time ago I saw this on the Internet: "Stem Cell Therapy to Treat Autism."

"Hey, honey!" I exclaimed from our office. "Sign Aidan up for honors English. They just found another cure for autism!"

Knowledge is power, but so is experience. I've finally learned to be patient and to put common sense forward before jumping headfirst into these so-called antidotes. Many of these websites have an uncanny way of making their products sound like cures without explicitly stating it. Most sites have wised up and replaced *cure* with *treatment*, but others are still trying to make a deceitful buck at another's expense. I discovered a long time ago that it's greed, not money, that is evil. Hence, these hoaxes infuriate me to no end.

On the flip side of all the alleged cures are the heartfelt stories of parents' journeys with their children's autism. For instance, YouTube has a three-minute movie, narrated by an autistic boy's father, about his son's experiences with autism from ages one to four. This brief excerpt is set to background music that creates a solemn mood for the viewer. Anyone with half a heart would be moved by what the father and his son shared.

I don't fault the Internet for its shortcomings, as it has provided us with valuable information that we otherwise wouldn't have encountered. What I do condemn is a person who tries to sell something useless to desperate parents.

34: Neurofeedback Therapy: Should We Try It?

I'VE BEEN LOOKING into something new for Aidan: neurofeedback therapy.

Here's an example of an online testimonial about this new treatment:

> Not all can connect to the challenges of life with autism. But most involved in its mystic world would love to have a type of therapy that has assured many of its life-changing capabilities. One such treatment for autism is neurofeedback.

> Take the situation with a seven-year-old boy named Joel, who appeared on a major network this past year. At a young age he was diagnosed with autism and had been discarded as socially and mentally inept. Joel's symptoms ranged from

extreme and frequent outbursts to a complete withdrawal from his surroundings. Yet, his parents refused to give up searching for a treatment plan to aid in his recovery.

Our neurofeedback organization worked with Joel forty-plus hours per week, and while his growth inched along, it did improve. In fact, it improved so much that in two years he started making friends and shined in his Boy Scout troop. Joel is now on his way to earning his Eagle Scout badge.

Take another experience with a ten-year-old girl named Susan. She had moderate comprehensible language and was very sensitive to loud noises. After 80 sessions of neurofeedback therapy, Susan excelled. Her speech dramatically improved, and her logic and reasoning increased. Susan greatly diminished her sensitivity to sounds and was delighted to attend her school's dance. She said she hoped to join her school's student council program in the near future as well.

Neurofeedback is a method of training the brain to function differently. In each session a therapist will attach small electrodes that conduct and transmit the electrical energy from the brain to various locations on the scalp.

The patient will then use brain waves to alter what is happening to a visual display on a computer screen. Through positive reinforcement, the brain learns to progressively use the desired waves, and ultimately changes in brain function may become permanent. Some consider it to be a video game for the brain.

Please note that a limited number of sessions may not positively treat a child with autism. Neurofeedback therapy can involve months and even years to have a significant effect. Neurofeedback isn't necessarily a cure, merely a way of getting the brain to function better.

Wow. Now that's some impressive material!

Are you kidding me, Kyle?! Haven't you learned anything by writing this book?

Yes, I hear you, *but*, while one side of me feels as though I should let all of this cure-all shyster stuff go by the wayside and merely enjoy our son with all his idiosyncrasies, I simply cannot seem to keep my eyes and ears closed to what else is out there.

Of course I know, deep down, that if something were *really* working for other folks, it would become such sensational news that everyone would be using it. But this disorder involves an extremely wide spectrum. What may not work for some may work for another. Right?

So what can I say? They've got me.

35: Lori and Me

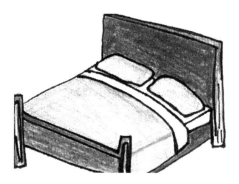

IN ADDITION TO the challenge of raising an autistic boy and two other children, I have found that sustaining a positive relationship with my wife has to be at the top of my priority list. Like the old saying goes, "If mama ain't happy, ain't nobody happy."

I know that might sound like a lot of mumbo jumbo, but it's absolutely true in my world. When I start feeling overwhelmed because I'm not meeting my fatherly expectations from my kids' needy points of view, I think of who was here first: my wife and me. Before Lori and I had a house, before we adored our lovable labs, before our kiddos, it was just us. We are the foundation that makes everything in our family work—or not work.

We've certainly experienced some strained times with the management of Aidan, not to mention our girls, but I've always attempted to stay clear of the thought of divorce. I read about a study showing that more divorces occur among parents of special-needs children than among parents of "normal" children. It's not too surprising. The way I figure it, we're in this together till the bitter and blissful end. I remember those vows I took oh-so-long ago—something about "for better and for worse." I do not doubt that some relationships became so stressed that splitting up seems to be the only viable option for the sanity of a family. But in my situation, I have never seen how getting divorced would make anything easier.

Still, I knew early on that it was going to take some extra effort to keep our family ship afloat. I needed to make every attempt to support Lori in being a happier person. Let's face it, she's the maternal one. I mow the lawn and *try* to fix things here and there; she tends to more tasks inside the house. When I lend a helping hand by folding the clothes and doing the dishes, she notices. She may not always pat me on the back and tell me I'm her Superman, but I know it gives her a break and she's become more relaxed because of it.

Unbeknownst to me at the time, I scored some personality points with my female colleagues by helping Lori out. They knew about my challenges with Aidan and asked how Lori was doing. I responded, "No matter what I do to help Lori, I know she does more than I do. If I can do more to make her life easier, she deserves it."

I've often asked myself: Who vacuums the house? Who plans the meals and does the shopping? Who cleaned the bathroom last? (Do I even know where the Windex is?) Who makes the kids' lunches? Who plans their parties? Who married *me*?

I have truly been in awe at some of the other activities that Lori has been able to manage outside of the home. As a volunteer aide in Aidan's classroom, she has done everything from working in the computer lab to organizing classroom art projects. She has attended the kids' field trips to the zoo and the pumpkin patch—and while she claimed these trips were fun, she also admitted that Aidan had a tough time with the rooster's *cock-a-doodle-doo* sound every five minutes (he adopted his usual on-edge expression and covered his ears with his hands). In addition to being superinvolved at Aidan, Riley, and Kira's school, she's been a substitute yard-duty monitor and hopes to become a full-time (paid) teacher's aide. I'm certainly aware that these jobs are laborious, but I feel comforted to know that Lori is available to our children while I'm at work.

Another important part of our relationship (and over-all life, for that matter) has been sleep time.

Man, I love sleep. If I could snooze like I did when I was in college, I'd be a refreshed piece of work. I look on those 2-a.m.-to-noon slumberfests as the sweet life. But now I've moved on to real-world responsibilities. I'm in daddy mode, and I'm up at the crack of dawn whether I choose to be or not. I haven't had to set my alarm clock since the birth of my first child.

Unfortunately, I have not been given the gift of restfulness in my advancing age. I'm not ready to claim myself as an insomniac, but I know exactly where my Ambien is located in the medicine cabinet. It usually takes me up to an hour to fall asleep after Lori does, and if I get up in the middle of the night (which is routine), it sometimes takes me another hour until I can slumber again.

Lori, on the other hand, is the best sleeper I know. She has great shut-eye genes in her family. Her father and brothers are infamous for dozing off on the couch in a roomful of relatives with a football game blasting on TV.

Lori is the master, though. She can fall asleep while sitting in a completely upright position on a rickety yellow school bus packed with kids. No joke! (Of course, it does help that we're always tired.) I am truly envious of this skill.

That being said, the sleep element is one of the important facets in our marriage. When we work together to get our troops down by 9:30 p.m, we're more successful in treating each other to extra niceties the next day.

We've also had to work on transparency. I don't tell lies, but there have been times when I didn't express how I was really feeling. I'm sure self-expression is hard for many guys, but I've learned one thing: it's all in the approach. When I've stepped up to the plate and spoken calmly and from the heart, we've been able to reconcile every matter. While my feelings haven't been expressed as deeply and as often as maybe they should have been, our relationship has improved and strengthened when I have.

And that brings us to Date Night. From time to time, I call the sitter (when I'm lucky enough to get one), make dinner reservations, and put on a collared shirt.

Even if it's just a burger and a cold one, Date Night is time alone that I've planned with my special one. Before the kids came along, it was just us two lovebirds sharing one milk shake with two straws. (Well, maybe we had our own milk shakes.) On our Date Nights, we do our best not to talk about the kids. We try to focus on our perfect vacation, a sweet job scenario, and what we'd do together if we won the lottery. Sharing these stories and dreams has made for great bonding and has given us a chance to smile a little more.

Then we inevitably go back to talking about the kids. They're on both of our minds anyway, and at least we have time to craft a game plan for when we get home and for tomorrow's family circus.

In closing, there's no doubt that Lori and I have shared our ups and downs. And despite the occasional tears and challenges in raising a special-needs boy and two spirited girls, I couldn't imagine a more fulfilling life partner for this unpredictable journey.

36: The True Heroes

WHEN I WAS as kid, I loved sports. Still do. Those guys on the field were my heroes back then, and I really looked up to them. But my perception of what makes a hero has changed radically since my youth.

I hereby acknowledge my new and improved champions:

To the occupational therapists: *I salute your valor*. To have the tolerance to allow my son to whine and complain about the simplest things, like not wanting to use the proper pencil grasp, yet not to give in to him, is truly inspiring.

To the Coach Jeffs, who take dozens of Sundays of their own time to provide a group of autistic children with opportunities to interact socially while engaging in a variety of physical activities: *I firmly shake your hand.*

To the special day teachers and classroom aides who have the ability to put their egos aside and get dirty with the kids: *I bow to you.* I am in awe of your work ethic and your tireless nature.

To the regular-education classroom teachers: *I applaud you* for fully including your special-needs students without condition. I get that your workload increases exponentially with these children in your classroom, and I highly appreciate your professionalism.

To the principals who make sincere attempts to provide a safe environment for socially challenged autistic students, despite the never-ending battles with bullying at your schools: *I stand at attention and in humble silence.*

To the special education coordinators from the district offices around the nation: *I sincerely thank you* for recognizing that parents of special-needs children aren't totally unreasonable. They simply want to give their children a chance to succeed like any other kid.

To the adapted physical education teachers (my mother among them) who spend their own money and work well past their caseload: *I drop to one knee* and offer you my deepest respect.

To the Mr. Kyles at all the My Gyms in the country: *I raise my largest pint of the finest lager* in honor of your full-of-life style, your childlike sense of humor, and the way you truly engage all children. You have made me want to be a better teacher.

To the ABA tutors with the patience of saints: *I tip my SF Giants cap to you.* How you diligently work with my son for four hours a day, twenty hours a week (some children get forty hours per week!), and not once roll your eyes at all his shortcomings is incredible. You are the backbone to my boy's success.

To the parents who never give up searching for new ways to support their special-needs children and never give up hope: *you ARE true heroes.*

And in case you weren't aware of this true hero, here's one to take note of too:

I recently finished reading a book entitled *The Game of My Life* by Jason "J-Mac" McElwain and Daniel Paisner. It's about an autistic boy named Jason (J-Mac) who hit six 3-pointers in the last three minutes and nine seconds of the only varsity basketball game he ever played in. He accomplished this monumental feat on Senior Night in front of a packed gym featuring a hometown crowd of family, friends, and fellow peers.

I mention this because I believe in these kinds of miracle stories. I believe that anyone—neurotypical or otherwise—can overcome insurmountable obstacles. This young man named J-Mac showed that with perseverance, hard work, dedication, and a simple love for a game, one can achieve greatness. He is a true inspiration and a hero!

37: The Interests of One Autistic Child

ONCE AIDAN TURNED two, it was clear he had particular interests. His main hobby, an autistic trait, was to line things up. Whether it was toy cars, puzzle pieces, or dominoes, he loved putting them in a long row on the floor.

A year later, his obsessive-compulsive interest veered toward trains. This was Aidan's passion. When he woke up in the morning, trains. When he returned from the park, trains. When we took our annual trip to Tahoe, trains. The boy loved his trains!

Within one week I must have made five wallet-thinning trips to the same toy shop, all in an effort to feed Aidan's fervor for those thrilling train tracks. The only complaint I had was Aidan's lack of perspective on the laws of physics. He'd get so frustrated when his custom-made mountain or bridge wouldn't quite hold its loose foundation. *CRASH!* The wooden pieces would tumble, and Aidan's wail would crank up to high.

By the age of three he developed his next fetish: puzzles.

We purchased six Melissa & Doug twelve-piece puzzle sets. Each of these cool puzzles came in its own wooden box with a user-friendly slide opening. Each time I came home from work, Aidan would have his half dozen jigsaw masterpieces proudly arranged (in a line, of course) on his bedroom floor. We later challenged Aidan with twenty-four-piece puzzles, and he rose to the occasion consistently—so much so that he would sometimes help his older sister with hers.

Around the age of four came the matching and memorization games. You know the game: place all cards facedown, turn over two cards, and search for a match. That kid would beat me almost every time!

And at five years old we were introduced to the Wii at Aidan's cousin's house. This video game system became an addiction like no other. For his sixth Christmas, Aidan received his very own Wii, which he was supposed to share with his sisters. With this stimulating activity, he obsesses about one game, playing it constantly until he masters it fully, and then moves on to the next one. Golf, Frisbee, baseball—you name it, he's the man! At age seven, he's in the midst of World 9 in *Super Mario Bros.,* if that means anything to Wii fans out there.

I believe the Wii also opened Aidan's eyes to a whole new and healthy world outside the house: sports. Our six-foot-high plastic basketball hoop gathered dust in Aidan's room for years after his birth. I later placed it outside, where it collected yard debris and rainwater. Then, from out of nowhere, the hoop's life force beamed in Aidan's direction and called to him like a beacon. And Aidan fed the hoop daily for months. Yes, he verbally and physically acted out a script from the Wii basketball game when he dribbled and shot the ball. But he was *playing outside with his dad*! This was monumental for us. (I would regularly ask him if he was playing the Wii or playing with his dad, so he would make some sense of our shared reality.)

This evolved into a basketball clinic with Kira at the local sports complex, which I discussed previously. And while his fanaticism recently faded, we still shoot a few hoops for fun.

Next came Ping-Pong, the cardio sport for the sloth at heart. And yes, Aidan's interest spawned from the Wii game. But what's a dad to do with his son's latest interest? Of course, I rushed right out and bought some cheap Ping-Pong paddles at Wal-Mart so we could tap that little white ball back and forth on our glass patio table.

After three Ping-Pong-filled days in a row, I knew this interest would last a while. So, I took my rudimentary know-how of Ping-Pong table making and bought a large piece of medium-density fiberboard at the hardware store. I cut it almost straight and laid it on top of our glass table. I could tell Aidan was fired up because he flashed his Christmas-morning smile. Priceless!

Feeding on his excitement, my self-diagnosed OCD kicked in again, and I took the weekend to spray-paint the fiberboard an emerald green—three coats of it. Aidan was beside himself as I struck my Captain Morgan pose (one foot on the table with a chivalrous grin).

The following day I bought some lacquer and white tape for the table lines, and we were ready for our first official Father-Son Ping-Pong Tournament. We rode the Ping-Pong bandwagon for the whole spring before delving into our next wave (no pun intended): swimming.

At seven years old, Aidan was legendary for his skillful dog-paddling around the pool with our two eager Labrador retrievers. His modified "Nestea plunge" (an adult-over-forty reference) was his signature delight, and diving for pennies ran a close second. We refreshed ourselves in the pool for a good seventy-five consecutive days before school knocked down our door and called for more structure in the Wilkin household.

The following spring, Aidan passed the official swim lap test, making him eligible to join our local parks and recreation swim team. And while he's not breaking any records, we are proud of our little man for participating in—and enjoying—an activity away from the TV.

Around this time Aidan's interest in wrestling with Dad intensified—so much so that my colleague, Mike (the high school's wrestling coach), convinced me to take Aidan for a trial run at a local wrestling camp for kids his age.

Mike said, "We have all kinds of kids in there. What do you have to lose? If he doesn't feel comfortable, you don't have to continue. Bring 'im by."

What I had to lose was a meltdown from Aidan—and a letdown for me. I'm a positive guy, but I couldn't help preparing myself for the worst. I imagined him refusing to be touched, throwing himself to the floor in tantrum-like fashion, and not comprehending any instruction. Well, I'm glad I put my reservations to the side and gave it a shot. Aidan made it through the first day without much conflict, and he shined at the next gathering. The sensory aspect of the rough-and-tumble workout and facilitated grappling was just what the OT doctor ordered. He seemed to love it, despite a random behavioral outburst or two.

To enhance the event, three students from my class were wrestling helpers in the clinic. They immediately found out who Aidan was (their teacher's son) and spent the next eight weeks guiding and supporting him. (I almost shed a tear at the luck I had with this one.)

And to add frosting to his already sugary cupcake, Aidan's friend Nick joined him. I admit I offered to be the driver to make Nick's experience that much more enticing to his parents, but Aidan ended up being the true benefactor. Relishing an activity he liked while spending time with his friend made the clinic all the more satisfying for him (and me!). I'm not sure he would have made it through the entire program without the assistance of my students and his school-yard chum.

While we do our best to keep up with Aidan's evolving interests, he also has his times when he sporadically hops from one activity to the next. Maybe this randomness stems from his autism. Or perhaps he's just an average little boy enjoying the next fling that presents itself. I'd like to think it's the latter.

38: Advice: Again, Just One Guy's Opinion

REALLY, WHO AM I to give advice? I'm a simple guy, with average intelligence, living on a fixed income, in a one-story house in Anytown, USA.

But what I *can* offer is a firsthand account of facing autism from a father's perspective. And based on my experiences, here are some words of wisdom.

1. Provide good commonsense parenting.

    Sometimes you need to throw out all the research and professional know-how and go with what feels right: your own intuition.

2. Demand good eye contact from your child.

Any child can gain from this character trait, but I've found that Aidan is clearly able to understand and carry out tasks more effectively if I have his undivided attention. Besides, this learned skill helps him to be socially polite, even though he may not actually be aware that he's doing it. I believe that our honing in on eye contact early has made Aidan appear more "normal" among his peers too.

3. Use timers.

We bought five cheap digital timers and distributed them around the house. (Trust me, you'll misplace a few.) With practically everything that Aidan did, we used to announce a countdown to help him make a smooth transition to the next activity.

For example, I'd say, "Aidan, I'm setting the timer for two minutes." I'd show him the timer and then say, "When it beeps, you will go brush your teeth." I'd make eye contact the entire time and have Aidan push the button on the timer himself so that he would be directly involved in the process.

Of course, folks who enjoy meltdowns and temper tantrums can keep doing what they're doing. I just couldn't take the drama anymore!

4. Use the phrase that has preserved our sanity: "First X, then Y."

To supplement the timer, we constantly use that statement with Aidan (and our other kids, for that matter). For example, if Aidan starts to play the Wii around bedtime, we'll say, "Aidan, *first* jammies, *then* the Wii." I also reach for a timer to establish a limit on his playing time. Otherwise, my turning the Wii off will be like someone abruptly pulling his hair.

I'll also check for a hint of understanding by peering into his blue eyes and saying, "Okaaayyy?"

"Okay," Aidan will reply, knowing I won't let him off the hook until he looks at me and says okay.

5. Learn from everybody—and from nobody.

When I entered the workforce in my teens, I met a guy who owned his own snow-blowing business in Chicago. He created this lucrative business from the ground up with no formal education. I asked this wise man how he'd made this all happen, and he said, "I am not successful because I'm smarter than everyone else. I am successful because I listen to what each person has to say. Every individual may have something of value that I can gain from."

As I have alluded to several times, no one person has all the right answers. Therefore, we've remained open to *all* the ideas of parents and guardians of autistic (and neurotypical) children. Some have worked, and others have fallen excruciatingly flat. But it reassures me that we have tried and tested multiple ideas in a real-world environment: our home.

Be leery of "professionals" who have merely discussed autism and its related issues from inside sterile clinical walls. Some of these people suggest strategies that seem like they've been lifted directly from a college textbook and aren't always the proven methods.

Thus, listen to many voices, but keep your common-sense filter in place. In the end, *you* are the best judge of what works for your child.

6. Adapt tactics or techniques to your own style.

Every autistic child is different, despite having the same label. Some of these children are totally verbal, and others do not talk at all. Some incessantly flap their hands when excited, while others blankly stare at even the most entertaining events.

Parents know their kids the best. They should decide how much to push and how much to pull (not literally, guys). I believe that the line where challenge meets frustration is the breaking point. Breakthroughs can happen there.

I know one parent who claimed his autistic child followed directions best if you got nose to nose and spoke in a strict tone (even for the simplest things). With Aidan, Lori and I actually held up an open picture frame to our faces and spoke through it to ask him questions. Both families had distinct and unconventional styles for getting their children to understand their instructions, and both had positive results.

And if your strategy is clickin' for you, don't worry about what the neighbors might think.

7. Show some gosh darn compassion for your kid, your mate, your family, and yourself! But don't expect others to.

Let's face it, everyone has challenges, and God knows parents of autistic children have them on a daily basis. So cut yourself some slack and know that you're a good person and that you're a superstar for never giving up and for keeping the faith.

And here are some closing thoughts from that simple guy you've been listening to for all these pages:

Love your family, because when it's all over, that's all that really matters.

CPSIA information can be obtained at www.ICGtesting.com
Printed in the USA
BVOW07s0837280813

329763BV00001B/66/P